"Many Christian resources focus either on biblical study to the neglect of deep personal life transformation or on life application based on a very flattened understanding of the gospel. World Harvest has drawn upon their history of rich gospel-based training to produce a series that targets real-life transformation grounded in a robust, grace-based theology. Only a resource saturated in the gospel can lead to the kind of meaningful life change promised to us in the Bible, and I am thrilled to see such a resource now available."

Rev. David H. Kim, Director of the Gotham Initiative, Redeemer Presbyterian Church, NYC

"I love the series of small group resources, *Gospel Identity*, *Gospel Growth*, and *Gospel Love*. They are theologically rich, but not stuffy; practical, but not pragmatic. They are life-transforming resources that will be used to transform communities on a mission with the gospel."

Scott Thomas, Pastor of Pastoral Development, The Journey Church

"This study brings a powerful experience of gospel truth and a personal relationship with Jesus and all those that he has placed in your life. Using biblical truths, written to open the eyes of all hearts to sins, and full of challenges by the Holy Spirit to change and grow, this is the study you need. User-friendly, even for a first time leader, it is progressive, time-sensitive, and will invite the most timid participant into heart application. I highly recommend this to all who are committed to growing closer to God and being a gospel tool to help others."

Nancy Puryear, Women's ministry director (more than eleven years), Christ Community Church; cross-cultural counselor

"God used Jack Miller to help Christians, and pastors especially, to recover the gospel of Jesus Christ as the functional core of the Christian faith. Jack's famous line, 'Cheer up, you're worse off than you think,' reopened the door to many of us with an invitation to drop the pretense of a good life and to admit and delight in our continuing, desperate need for Jesus. As a church planter and trainer of church planters, I have often wished for a concise series of Bible studies that would help churches to not only know this gospel of grace, but to experience it as well. That's precisely what this series of gospel studies offers. It is a great way to biblically and relationally ground Christians in the gospel of Jesus Christ, and I heartily recommend it."

John F. Thomas, PhD, Director of Glob to City

"I'm probably the most 'religious' person you know. I make my living teaching religious students (in seminary) to be more religious, doing religious broadcasts, writing religious books, and preaching religious sermons. It's very easy to lose the 'main thing' about the Christian faith in a religious morass. These studies remind me that it's all about Jesus, and Jesus is all about the Good News (the gospel). They are refreshing, informative, and life changing. In fact, these studies are like a refreshing drink of cold, pure water to a thirsty man. Read and use these books from World Harvest Mission and get out of the way as you listen to the laughter and relief of the redeemed."

Steve Brown, Key Life radio broadcaster; author of *Three Free Sins: God Isn't Mad at You*

"*Gospel Love* is unique in that it works at the very heart of our faith. It is a marriage course, a discipleship course, and a Bible study, but it is so much more. It is all about getting the central passion of Christianity—the cross of Jesus Christ—at the center of your life. And not just your thinking life, but your doing and experiencing life. So it is good theology and good practice combined. If you get the cross right, then everything else works."

Paul Miller, Director of SeeJesus (www.seeJesus.net); author of *A Praying Life*

"I've dated a lot of different curriculum in the past, but there's very little worth taking home to meet Mom. Too often, the writing is too high (too theoretical—have you actually met a sinner before?), too emotive (talk to my head and my heart!), or too clunky (really? can I accomplish this in a week—much less an evening?). WH's new Gospel Series small group materials are rifle-ready for the foot soldier in the church to use without a lot of training, and they seem to have been written by real sinners/ strugglers for fellow sinners/strugglers. Thanks, WHM, for something I can actually use!"

Geoff Bradford, Pastor, Christ the King Presbyterian Church, Raleigh, NC

GOSPEL LOVE

GOSPEL LOVE

GRACE, RELATIONSHIPS, AND EVERYTHING THAT GETS IN THE WAY

Book Three in the
Gospel Transformation Series

Serge

New
Growth
Press

www.newgrowthpress.com

Gospel Love: Grace, Relationships, and Everything that Gets in the Way

New Growth Press, Greensboro, NC 27404
www.newgrowthpress.com
Copyright © 2012 by Serge.

Gospel Love: Grace, Relationships, and Everything that Gets in the Way is based on portions of discipleship material developed at World Harvest Mission by Paul E. Miller which was used as the basis for *Gospel Transformation* (copyright © 2001 by World Harvest Mission) written by Neil H. Williams.

Typesetting: Lisa Parnell, lparnell.com
Cover Design: Faceoutbooks, faceoutstudio.com

ISBN 978-1-936768-74-5

Printed in China

23 22 21 20 19 18 17 16   5 6 7 8 9

CONTENTS

INTRODUCTION

Welcome to *Gospel Love: Grace, Relationships, and Everything that Gets in the Way*! This study is designed to help you discover how your identity and growth in Jesus is inextricably tied to your relationships—both inside and outside the church.

In *Gospel Love*, the third and final study in the "Gospel Transformation" series, you'll learn how the gospel of Jesus Christ frees you to actively love and accept everyone God puts in your path—because those people *are* your path. You'll learn that you're part of a new family—the body of Christ. You'll discover what living incarnationally looks like, exploring the importance of love in community; loving and forgiving those who are difficult to love; extending grace in our relationships; loving honestly, even in conflict; learning about the role of the Spirit in growing the body of Christ; and finally, exploring opportunities to extend your new family by bringing the gospel to others.

As you work through *Gospel Love*, as well as the other two books in the "Gospel Transformation" series—*Gospel Identity: Discovering Who You Really Are* and *Gospel Growth: Becoming a Faith-Filled Person*—you'll be encouraged to lead a life of greater faith, repentance, and love. If you haven't yet completed the first two books, we encourage you to do so before beginning *Gospel Love*. *Gospel Identity* and *Gospel Growth* lay a foundation for *Gospel Love*, as they address how finding our identity in Jesus Christ and living in dependence on him equip us with what we need to love others.

So, how does "gospel transformation" occur? How does it relate to life? What *are* the essentials of the Christian life, and how do they change us? That's what this series is all about. Let's summarize it in four foundational points that we'll return to again and again.

1. Cheer up! The gospel is far greater than you can imagine! The gospel of Jesus Christ—and his power to transform our lives and relationships, communities, and ultimately, the nations—is the best news we will ever hear. It gives us a new identity, not based on race, social class, gender, theology, or a system of rules and regulations, but on faith in Jesus. And it's an identity that defines every aspect of our lives. Because of this we no longer have to hide from our sin and pretend we have it all together. We now have a new way to live and relate to God and others, every day. The good news is not only relevant to us when we first believe, but it continues to work in us and through us as we continue to believe, visibly expressing itself in love (Galatians 5:6).

2. Cheer up! You are worse than you think! One of the great hindrances to Christian growth, healthy relationships, and strong communities is a life of pretense—pretending that we don't struggle with a multitude of sins, such as self-righteous attitudes, foul tempers, nagging anxieties, lustful looks, controlling and critical hearts, and a general belief that we are better than other people. Part of the good news is that God knows all this—knows *us*—already, and he wants to change us. Because our sin blocks our intimacy with God and others, we need God's Spirit to show us our many fears and offensive ways, and we need the insights of others to encourage us and speak into our lives.

Our first two points work together in a cyclical fashion. On the one hand, none of us wants to look at our sin without knowing the good news of forgiveness and deliverance from it. On the other hand, our view of the gospel is severely limited if we do not continually see the depths of our sin. The gospel cannot soak deeply into us unless it addresses our ongoing need for it. And that brings us to our next point.

3. Cheer up! God's Spirit works in your weakness! We not only have a new identity, but we have been given the Spirit who is more than sufficient to lead, guide, and empower us in our new life. The power that raised Jesus from the dead is at work in our new lives as well (Ephesians 1:19–20). Nevertheless, the power of the Spirit does not work automatically, but through repentant, obedient faith. Furthermore, this power is made evident through our weakness (2 Corinthians 12:9; 13:4). Along with Paul, we can delight in our weakness, for then we are strong and God is glorified. The result is a wonderful freedom to forget about ourselves and stop wondering whether we have enough ability—we don't. But we can rejoice in the knowledge that God uses and empowers the weak. Therefore, we have the hope discussed in point four.

4. Cheer up! God's kingdom is more wonderful than you can imagine!
The kingdom of God is the new and final age that began with Jesus' coming. It is the age of righteousness, peace, and joy in the Holy Spirit (Romans 14:17). The kingdom of God is about the renewing of all things, and God has made us a part of this great story of salvation. This kingdom is about the reconciliation of relationships, about the restoration of justice and equality, about freedom from every lord except Jesus, about forgiveness, and about the defeat of Satan. It is about compassion for the poor and powerless, about helping those who are marginalized and rejected by society, and about using our gifts and resources for the advancement of others. It is about new communities and the transformation of society and culture. For Paul, to preach the gospel is to preach the kingdom, and therefore to preach the whole counsel of God (Acts 20:24–27).

The goal of each study, therefore, is not simply to master the content, but to allow the gospel to master you and your group more fully. Knowledge is like bread—unless it is digested, it will go stale. The content of this course needs to be chewed, digested, and assimilated, so that true *spiritual* growth can occur. It's easy to slip into the routine of just completing the lesson, but don't. Our ultimate goal here is love—love rooted in a growing faith in Jesus, which leads to more love (Galatians 5:6).

Our prayer is that through your time together, your love for Jesus, and the people God brings into your life, you will grow deeper daily. May God bless and encourage your group as you work together through this study!

ABOUT THE SESSIONS

The sessions in this study are built to take 75 minutes apiece. They've been built so there's plenty of good content, but also plenty of room for discussion. There are suggested times for each section, but again do what you need to as a group—the goal isn't to master the content, but to allow the gospel to master you and your group.

Sessions follow a logical order, so be sure to cover them in the sequence given. Often, one session builds on what has been previously covered in the session or sessions before it. Furthermore, each session follows its own sequence so that your group can get the most impact from it. Each time you get together you can expect to see the following:

Overview—This introduction of the session includes the one point to take away from the session. Reading it as part of your group time is optional, but by stating the focus up front everyone knows what's coming.

Opening the Discussion—In this brief opening section, take time to unwind and transition from your previous environment (home, work, or some other place) and into the theme of the session. The questions here are intended to help the entire group interact. They also help set up what comes later in the session. And maybe, because you are so busy having a good time discussing a "light" question, you won't even realize you've already gotten down to business.

Opening the Word—This is the heart of each session, and typically the longest section. You'll spend some serious time digging into God's Word and discovering its meaning in ways you hadn't before. More importantly, you'll discover how the information you're studying applies to your life right now, and what God wants to do with it.

Opening Your Life—In this closing section you'll move from *understanding how* the Bible applies to your life to actually *applying* it. At the end of each session you will break into smaller groups or pairs to share how you will apply that day's lesson—and to commit to following up with each other during the week. This way everyone's involved, engaged, and committed to one another. The lesson will usually give some suggestions for its application, but if God is telling you to do something else, *go for it*!

In short, in each session you'll be challenged to share, to think, and to act. And as you do, gospel transformation will be more than just the title of a Bible study series. It will be a reality you live every day.

FOR LEADERS

We strongly suggest working through each session on your own first, prior to your group time. Your prep time shouldn't require more than one-half hour, but take as much time as you need. Your goal is the same as your group's—to grow in faith, repentance, and obedience. As you review the material, honestly answer each question. Ask the Spirit to reveal your own heart, and be prepared to share what the Spirit reveals with the group, as long as it's appropriate. Your own transparency and vulnerability will open the door for others.

You'll notice that there are times during the session (especially during "Opening Your Life") when we suggest getting into pairs or smaller groups. Feel free to do this at other times during the session when we haven't explicitly told you to do so. It's a great way to make sure everyone remains engaged with the material and with each other, and it frees people to share about matters they may not want to discuss with the entire group.

Also, in the back of the book are suggested answers and reflections relating to each session's questions. Don't use this section as a crutch or a shortcut. Wrestle with each question and passage on your own and as a group. Figure out its meaning for yourselves. Then, if you like, look in back to add further insight to your discussion time.

Finally, here are some expectations we encourage you to have for your group members, and to share openly with them:

1. **Expect to be challenged.** The answers will not come quickly or easily. If they do, we haven't done our job properly. As you work through each question, expect that it will take some time, thought, and soul-searching to complete each session.

2. **Expect the Holy Spirit** to be the one ultimately responsible for the growth of your group, and for the change in each person's life—including your own. Relax and trust him.

3. **Expect your group time together** to include an open, give-and-take discussion of each session's content and questions. Also expect times of prayer at each meeting. In fact, plan for them.

4. **Expect struggle.** Don't be surprised to find in your group a mixture of enthusiasm, hope, and honesty, along with indifference, anxiety, skepticism, and covering up. We are all people who need Jesus every day, so expect your group to be made up of people who wrestle with sin and have problems—just like you!

5. **Expect to be a leader** who desires to serve, but who needs Jesus as much as the rest of the group. No leader should be put on a pedestal or be expected to have the right answers. Give yourself the freedom to share openly about your own weaknesses, struggles, and sins. Covet your group's prayers.

6. **Expect confidentiality**, and be prepared to ask the group to make that commitment with you. Anything personal must be kept in confidence and never shared with others outside the group. Gossip will quickly destroy a group.

You are ready to begin. May God bless your group's journey together!

TURNING FAITH INTO LOVE

OVERVIEW

In this session we'll explore the importance of loving others and its rootedness in faith.

Genuine faith and repentance move us away from ourselves and into the lives of other people. In this session we'll explore that truth and its practical implications. Another aim of this session is to demonstrate that this love flowing from faith is the only thing that has value. Although there are many commands to love, these commands don't have any power of themselves to bring about change. Put simply, we can't do it ourselves. Only through faith, repentance, and the Spirit can we hope to become the kinds of people God intends us to become.

OPENING THE DISCUSSION

1. When have you faced a task you *knew* you couldn't accomplish on your own? How did it get done? What did you learn from that experience?

In learning about our new community in Christ, we must remember how important our relationships have already been to us. As we saw in our last session, our faith expresses itself in love, and we can show that love much more together than we can separately. At the same time, there's another relationship we dare not forget as we do this. We can accomplish nothing for God without the Spirit working in our community, expressing his desires for us through love, faith, and repentance. So let's explore how we can make our love for others more real.

OPENING THE WORD

Have volunteers read Romans 13:8–10 and Galatians 5:13–16, and then discuss the following questions:

2. What does Paul mean when he says that love fulfills (or sums up) the law?

3. How does serving others free us from the desires of our flesh—whether it's our desire to indulge (Galatians 5:13) or our tendency to bite and devour each another (Galatians 5:15)?

Have a couple more volunteers read Galatians 5:6 and James 2:14–26, and then discuss the following questions:

4. How do we see "faith expressing itself through love" (Galatians 5:6) in the passage from James?

"How many are called physicians, who know not how to heal! How many are called watchers, who sleep all night long! So, many are called Christians, and yet in deeds are not found such; because they are not this which they are called, that is, in life, in manners, in faith, in hope, in charity."
— St. Augustine, "Homilies on the First Epistle of John"

Take a minute or two to read through the following list of principles, either silently or aloud, and then discuss the questions that follow:

Five Principles of Faith and Love

Principle 1: The type of love God desires cannot operate without faith. The dynamics of faith and love cannot be separated. Love does not stand or operate in isolation. Without faith, love is nothing.

Principle 2: The opposite is also true. Faith cannot be present without love. No one can claim to have faith, and yet show no love.

Principle 3: In the dynamic of faith working through love, the starting point must always be faith. With the cart (love) before the horse (faith), nothing works. We cannot forget about faith as we try to love. Faith feeds love. Faith is the trigger, the spark, the ignition. If love runs out of fuel it fails.

Principle 4: Although faith works through love, we often discover our failure of faith when we examine the details of a particular situation where we have failed to love. In other words, the conviction of the Holy Spirit often begins with a failure to love. It is difficult to know whether we are living by faith apart from seeing fruit or lack of it. Lack of love always indicates unbelief, or a lack of faith. Therefore, it is difficult, if not downright impossible, to see our unbelief without seeing our lack of love. We usually have to work backwards from a failure to love to find a failure of faith. This type of analysis helps us realize a bigger problem than simply "I didn't love." It also asks, "What did I *really* believe?" and "Where was my sin against God and him alone?"

Principle 5: We can own up to our lack of love only when we are appropriating the truth of the gospel into our lives, that is, resting by faith in God's love for us. Just as we can easily be deceived about our faith (and thus ask ourselves "Are we loving?"), we are also easily deceived about our love (and thus ask ourselves "Are we believing?"). Apart from trust in God, we will resist exposing our lack of love and our need for change. Apart from faith, we will think that our evil words and actions are actually showing love to others. For example, you might think "speaking the truth in love" means "As long as I speak the truth (about what *you* are like and how *you* should change), I'm being a loving person." Just as we are often deceived about our faith, we are often fooled about our love.

5. Why does faith *have* to express itself through love? What's the connection? (See principles 1 and 2.)

6. Why must we begin with faith in order to have love? (See principle 3.)

7. Why is it difficult to see a failure of faith until we first see a failure of love? When has the Spirit convicted you on this point—or how does he now? (See principle 4.)

8. Think about a time when you *did* all the right things for someone, but not in a loving way. What were the results? Why? (See principle 5.)

OPENING YOUR LIFE

*If love fulfills the demands of the law, yet faith comes before love, then we had better understand God's definition of love **and** its relation to faith. So let's look now at **the** love chapter.*

Read aloud 1 Corinthians 13:1–13. Then discuss the following questions:

9. If—as we determined above—faith comes before love, why is love more important than faith (v. 13)?

10. Think of a person or group of people whom God has called you to love. Now take yourself out of the equation for a minute as we discuss the following question: If someone else were doing it, what would you say love in action should look like in that situation?

11. Now insert yourself back into that situation. Realistically—not ideally—what would *your* love in action look like in that situation? What, if anything, do you need to let the Spirit change in you to make that happen?

Have group members get into pairs.

Take ten minutes to review this week's challenges and share which one you'll take on—or whether you'll take on something else God has prompted you to do instead. Also make plans to touch base with each other before the next session. In the space that follows, write what you're doing in response to this week's session.

- Ask the Spirit to show you where you're failing to believe and love. What are a couple of areas in your life where you see a failure of love reflecting a failure of faith? What practical steps can you take to address it?

- Turn your faith into love this week. Come up with a practical way to show compassion to someone in need—if at all possible, someone who doesn't know Jesus. Fill a gas tank, buy a hot meal, or just provide a listening ear. Commit to do something meaningful that requires your intentional time and effort.

- Think again about the person(s) God is calling you to love in questions 10 and 11. What is one practical thing you can do this week to love them better? Your group may even want to consider loving others through doing an event together. Plan something fun such as a cookout, Super Bowl party, game night, or holiday celebration. Invite your not-yet Christian (*and* Christian) friends, family members…*whoever* God has placed on your heart during this session. Make it a time to celebrate God's love, and your love for each other (even those you're meeting for the first time!).

This week I'll "convert" my faith into love by:_____

_____

_____

_____

After ten minutes get back together and close in prayer. Pray something like this:

> *Dear God, We ask that you would help us gain a deeper appreciation of your love for us—even in those places where we have trouble fully trusting you. As we understand your love more deeply, we ask that each of us would know how to show it to those we care most about. In Jesus' name, amen.*

ADDITIONAL NOTES:

WE'RE IN THIS TOGETHER

OVERVIEW

In this session we'll grow in awareness that we're part of a new community—one comprised of all who are in Christ.

Our redemption in Christ brings us into a new community of believers. As we are united to Christ, so we become united to one another. This community is as important to us as a pile of fiery coals are to an individual piece of coal. Separating ourselves from the community of believers only invites coldness. Life in the new community is the opposite of selfishness.

The manifestations of our new life in Christ—the fruit of the Spirit, the increased imitation of Christ—only have meaning and value as they are lived out in the context of this new community. It is *in* this community that we express these things outwardly to one another, and it is *through* this community that we express these things outwardly to the world.

OPENING THE DISCUSSION

Leader: How you start today's session depends on how well you already know one another as a group:

- **If this is your first time together as a group** take some time to get comfortable. Don't "jump right into the session" (even though that is what you will actually be doing). Give everyone the opportunity to relax first. Engage in a bit of small talk. After about five minutes, ask everyone to introduce themselves, and take a few moments to share what you're each hoping to get out of this study.

- **If you're an existing group, and have a social time before starting** tell everyone you'll be starting the session promptly today—then just go on with your normal social time. You might get some quizzical looks, but you're also setting up this session's message perfectly.

Once your "social time" is done, discuss the following questions:

1. How does spending time together help people loosen up and become comfortable with one another? What else do we do to help lower our guards with each other?

2. What keeps us from relaxing and "being real" around other Christians? Why?

Leader: The sections *in italics* are for you, to help you and your group transition from one part of the session to the next. Read them verbatim, put what's here in your own words, or just move on to the next section—whatever works best for you and your group.

---

*The Bible tells us that we're all fallen people. We're going to let each other down. It's inevitable. We're **all** lost causes without Jesus. Nonetheless—or maybe, therefore—Jesus has called **all** of us as Christians to love one another.*

*Furthermore, we're not simply to pursue relationships **with** other Christians, but to pursue Jesus—and the world he sends us out to—together **as** Christians. When Christ is our focus, the little things that can get in the way in our relationships don't seem so important. When we pursue Jesus together, our relationships naturally become closer, deeper, and more loving, because Jesus now sets the tone. And Jesus is never going to steer us the wrong way. Let's begin exploring how this can become more of a reality in our lives.*

"All the blessings we enjoy are Divine deposits, committed to our trust on this condition, that they should be dispensed for the benefit of our neighbors."
— John Calvin, *Institutes of the Christian Religion*

OPENING THE WORD

Have volunteers read Romans 12:3–16; Ephesians 4:1–6, 11–16. Then discuss the following questions:

3. Based on what you've just read, why is it important to remember we're the *body* of Christ?

4. What makes us a body? In other words, what provides the foundation for our union with other believers in Christ (see especially Ephesians 4:4–5)?

5. Given this foundation, how are we to live? Give examples, from these passages.

Let's explore that last question further.

6. Take turns reading aloud through the list of Scripture passages below. After reading each passage, identify one activity of the body of Christ presented there, and then come up with at least one practical example of how this activity could be done in community.

- Matthew 28:18–20
- Romans 15:26
- 2 Corinthians 1:3–5
- Ephesians 5:19

- Philippians 4:6
- Hebrews 3:13
- James 1:27
- 1 John 1:7

7. Several of these activities can be done on one's own. How does doing them in community change how they're done? How does it affect their potential impact?

8. In what ways do you isolate yourself from your faith community rather than engage with it? Why?

OPENING YOUR LIFE

Take a minute or two to read through "The New Community in Christ" illustration, which gives a sampling from what's known as the "one anothering" passages of the Bible. Afterward, we'll discuss.

Figure 1.1

The New Community in Christ

love...
John 13:34

sing to...   pray for...   encourage...
Ephesians 5:19   James 5:16   Hebrews 3:13

do not judge...   greet...   do not slander...
Romans 14:13   1 Peter 5:14   James 4:11

agree with...   confess your sins to...   teach...
1 Corinthians 1:10   James 5:16   Romans 15:14

ONE ANOTHER

show compassion to...   be humble with...
Zechariah 7:9   1 Peter 5:5

submit to...   care for...   build up...
Ephesians 5:21   1 Corinthians 12:25   Romans 14:19

bear with...   forgive...   accept...
Colossians 3:13   Ephesians 4:32   Romans 15:7

honor...
Romans 12:10

9. Which of these "one anothers" stood out to you? Why do you think that is?

10. What do you need to receive from Christ in order to build the type of community described in the "one another" passages?

11. After considering everything we've looked at today, how do you think you need to become reengaged, or more deeply engaged, with the faith communities you're connected with—your church, ministries, this group? How do you think your participation in your faith community helps you respond differently to the other relationships in your life?

Subdivide into groups of three or four.

*Let's think more about our answers to that last question and about the next steps each of us can take to make that real in our lives. Each week you'll get the opportunity to respond to what God wants to do in your life. Below you'll find a few options to help you think through how to put what you've learned today into practice. Choose one of these ways to step out in faith, so that you really have to rely on Christ—or if God has prompted you to do something else through this session, by all means do **that**!*

*In the space that follows, write the one thing you'll do this week to apply today's lesson to your life. Take ten minutes to share about your choices with your group, and then make plans to touch base with each other before the next session, to check in and encourage one another. Your touch-base time can be face-or-face, by phone, or online, but make a commitment you can keep—and then **keep** it.*

- Look at the "one-anothering" diagram again. This week do a little exercise: *Outside* the circle, write down the opposite (or "evil twin") of each characteristic. For example, write "lord it over someone" instead of "submit to." You'll end up with a word-picture of the characteristics that destroy community. Then take time to pray about the word picture you've created, which evil twins you're susceptible to, and what God wants to change in you and how.

- Become involved in some aspect of your faith community, preferably one that has not been a regular part of your life, or perhaps one that would be a challenge for you. Contact someone who can help you get connected.

- Come up with a service project your entire group can do *outside* of church. Go on a lawn-mowing, leaf-raking, or snowplowing expedition, or team up with an organization that builds houses for the needy—whatever works for your group. Afterward, discuss how your time together both helped others and drew you closer together as group. Consider ways you might make this a regular occurrence.

This week I'll help build the community I'm in by: _____

_____

_____

_____

After ten minutes get back together and close in prayer. Pray something like this:

> *Dear God, Thank you for the relationships that already exist within our group. We ask for wisdom on how to both grow these relationships and extend them past the boundaries of our group, to love the world you send each one of us into. In Jesus' name, amen.*

ADDITIONAL NOTES:

I HAVE TO LOVE THEM?

OVERVIEW

In this session we'll recognize that the ultimate expression of love is toward those who are difficult to love. We'll also identify some of the barriers we face as we attempt to express that kind of love.

This session will deal primarily with the barriers we create to loving others. Before considering these obstacles we'll look at one particular area that exemplifies the depth and manner of love that ought to characterize us: love for those who are difficult to love.

The rest of the lesson will concentrate on various barriers to love, including the following:

- lack of vulnerability;

- confusing imitation fruit with genuine fruit;

- placing conditions on our love;

- avoiding the "messiness" of love; and

- persecution and suffering.

OPENING THE DISCUSSION

Leader: In preparation for this session, gather paper scraps for everyone to write on. Everyone will also need something to write with and a small bowl. You will use all these items during "Opening Your Life."

---

1. Think about a time when your first impressions of someone turned out to be totally wrong (in a good way). What initially "turned you off" to that person? What happened to change your perspective?

*It's easy to like people who like us, or to like those we have things in common with. But let's face it: it's hard to like someone who, intentionally or not, has offended us or puts up a barrier between us. And sometimes, intentionally or not, **we're** the ones putting up the barriers.*

However, Jesus doesn't just call us to love the people we like. God loves and accepts each of us in our weaknesses and our faults, and through that love changes us. And if God can change us, he can change anyone. So let's expand our field of vision and our hearts, so we can better see and love others the way Jesus sees and loves them— starting with the hardest cases we'll face.

OPENING THE WORD

Have volunteers read Matthew 5:38–48 and Romans 12:14–21. Then discuss:

2. How are we to respond to those who are difficult to love? What are some of the reasons both Jesus and Paul give for why we should respond this way?

Not everyone that's hard to love is an enemy. But that doesn't mean they're easy for us to love. The problem, however, isn't just them or even mostly them—it's us. Let's look at the barriers we put up to avoid loving others, and how we might start breaking those barriers down.

Barrier 1: Lack of vulnerability

Have a volunteer read Mark 15:29–32. Then discuss these questions:

3. What's the connection between love and vulnerability? How does Jesus show that here?

4. What challenges do we face when we make ourselves vulnerable to others?

"To love at all is to be vulnerable. Love anything, and your heart will certainly be wrung and possibly be broken. . . . The only place outside Heaven where you can be perfectly safe from all the dangers and perturbations of love is Hell."
— C. S. Lewis, *The Four Loves*

Barrier 2: Confusing imitation fruit for genuine fruit

Have a volunteer read Revelation 3:1–3, and then discuss the following questions:

5. How does one develop a reputation of being alive, although one is dead? When have you seen this happen?

Barrier 3: Placing conditions on our love

Read Matthew 5:46–47, and then discuss the following question:

6. What are some conditions that you place on loving others, especially those close to you, such as a child, spouse, or close friend?

Barrier 4: Avoiding the "messiness" of love

Have volunteers read 2 Corinthians 6:3–10 and Hebrews 4:14–15. Then discuss the following questions:

7. What are some ways that temptation or suffering—or the threat of them—hinders our love for others? What assurance do we have to counter those threats?

Barrier 5: Persecution and suffering

Take a few minutes to read the following excerpt by Corrie ten Boom, either silently or aloud. Then discuss the question that follows.

Radical Love

A wonderful example of love in the face of suffering is seen in the lives of Corrie ten Boom and her sister Betsie. While imprisoned in a Nazi concentration camp, they learn that it was a man named Jan Vogel who had betrayed them and many others to the Gestapo. Corrie confessed she was so angry that if she came face-to-face with this man, she could kill him. In her aching rage and resentment, she could not pray. She writes:

> What puzzled me all this time was Betsie. She had suf-fered everything I had and yet she seemed to carry no burden of rage. "Betsie!" I hissed one dark night when I knew that my restless tossing must be keeping her awake. Three of us now shared this single cot as the crowded camp received new arrivals. "Betsie, don't you feel anything about Jan Vogel? Doesn't it bother you?"

> "Oh yes, Corrie! Terribly! I've felt for him ever since I knew—and pray for him whenever his name comes to mind. How dreadfully he must be suffering!"

> For a long time I lay silent in the huge shadowy barracks restless with the sighs, snores, and stirrings of hundreds of women. Once again I had the feeling that this sister with whom I had spent all my life belonged to another order of beings. Wasn't she telling me in her gentle way that I was as guilty as Jan Vogel? Didn't he and I stand together before an all-seeing God convicted of the same sin of murder? For I had murdered him with my heart and with my tongue.

> "Lord Jesus," I whispered into the lumpy ticking of the bed, "I forgive Jan Vogel as I pray that You will forgive me.

I have done him great damage. Bless him now, and his family…" That night for the first time since our betrayer had a name I slept deep and dreamlessly until the whistle summoned us to roll call. (Corrie ten Boom, *The Hiding Place*)

8. What's your response to this passage? What do you think it would take for you to have the kind of love Betsie—and later, Corrie—had for Jan Vogel?

OPENING YOUR LIFE

Give everyone a scrap of paper and a pen or pencil. Ask everyone to think about a time they felt rejected or judged by others, for *whatever* reason. Have them write a word or phrase on their slips of paper describing how that experience felt, then fold their papers and drop them in your bowl. Then pass the bowl around and let everyone take one of the folded scraps, making sure they don't get their own scrap. Have everyone read their scraps aloud, and then discuss the following questions:

9. What was harder—writing what you wrote or having it read aloud? Why?

10. What do these words tell you about how it feels when *other* people are judged?

Have a volunteer read 1 Corinthians 1:25–31.

11. How does this passage help put things in perspective—both in terms of how God sees and loves you and how you should see and love others?

12. How can you train yourself to see past your barriers to loving others, and instead to see and love them the way Jesus does?

Ask everyone to get into pairs.

Take ten minutes to review this week's challenges and share which one you'll take on—or whether you'll take on something else God has prompted you to do instead. Also make plans to touch base with each other before the next session. In the space that follows, write what you're doing in response to this week's session.

- What barriers come between you and others? Which one comes up the most? Figure out what *your* "signature barrier" is, and then begin addressing it this week. For instance, if you hate cigarette smoking, join coworkers during their smoking break. (You don't have to smoke, of course; just love the people who *do*.) Or listen to a political talk show that you normally avoid. Humanize the people who don't share your views, and think about how you can love them. Breaking down a barrier may be as simple as spending time with someone you are called to love and really listening to them and paying attention to their needs.

- Befriend a neighbor who doesn't belong to your social or economic class, religion, or race. Don't make a "mission" out of it—just get to know the person. Afterward, reflect on the experience. How did your perceptions change? How will it change the way you approach your neighbors (and others you feel are somehow different from you) in the future?

- Neighbors aren't always people you know! So this week, as a group, find some new neighbors. It may be the elderly people at the grocery store who need help getting groceries to the car, the poor or homeless in your town, or those teenagers in your neighborhood who clearly are looking for something better to do. Ask God to open your eyes to all the people in your life that are so easy to overlook, but who still need to be loved well.

This week I'll let God break down my barriers to loving others by:

_____

_____

_____

Bring everyone back together after 10 minutes.

Let's take this one step further. This session may have stirred up memories that make you realize that someone's judgment has hurt you more deeply than you'd thought. Or perhaps you have a new understanding of how your own judgments and refusals to love have hurt others. Let's take a minute or so to reflect silently, and then we'll close in prayer. If there's something you want to ask God's help for out loud, though, please don't be afraid to do so. We won't judge you.

After at least a minute of silence, pray something like the following:

> Lord, your Word tells us, "Do not condemn and you will not be condemned" (Luke 6:37). We want to obey you. But we've all been guilty of judging others at one time or another. We don't want to be defined by—or in bondage to—who or what we like or don't like, or what we're for or against. We want to be defined by **you**. Forgive us for judging others and withholding love from them. Help us see them through your eyes. Open our eyes so we can really see others, and **love** others, the way you've called us to—the way you already love **us**. Amen.

LAY DOWN THE LAW ... AND LEAVE IT THERE

OVERVIEW

In this session we'll recognize some of the many ways we use laws or rules for wrong purposes, and how to instead extend grace in our relationships.

As we've already seen, the gospel works itself out in relationships. This session exposes an area that perennially creates havoc in those relationships—the abuse of laws. We often abuse, and sometimes create, laws as grabs for power, control, identity, authority, or just self-protection. We can make laws or rules based on our own idolatry and try to impose them on others to bring about "blessings." We can use laws and rules for wrong purposes and for selfish reasons.

The irony of all this is that when we use laws in wrong ways, we become lawbreakers—even of our own rules. Ultimately, our rules say more about ourselves than about others.

OPENING THE DISCUSSION

10 MINUTES

1. What's one rule you encountered when growing up—whether at home, school, or elsewhere—that just seemed…well, dumb? Does that rule make any more sense to you now? Explain.

We've all encountered rules that seem questionable, even if they once made sense to someone at some time. We can probably even look back at some of our childhood rules and laugh now. However, we're often guilty of the same thing in our lives right now. We create rules to help us live better—or to "help" others live better—that end up bringing bondage instead of grace to ourselves and others. Let's examine how this happens, and what we can do to stop it.

OPENING THE WORD

45 MINUTES

Divide into three subgroups and assign to each one the following passages: Mark 3:1–6; Luke 7:36–50; and John 12:1–7. Take ten minutes to read the assigned passage and discuss the following questions:

Leader: Divide into more than three subgroups if necessary to keep no more than five people in each small group. Just assign the same passage to more than one group.

---

2. What false law did the people in your passage try to enforce? What motivated them?

3. What is Jesus' reaction? What truer law did Jesus indicate was being broken, as he refuted the false law?

Bring everyone back together after ten minutes. Have a representative from each group share insights from their discussion time.

Our false laws reveal both a lack of love toward others and a lack of trust (and love) toward God. Read through the following three lists of "commandments." As you read through each list, circle any commandments you've found yourself using, and add two or three examples of demanding statements that you've given, heard, or received. We'll discuss afterward.

Figure 4.1

"Commandments" for our friends

I	"With friends like you, who needs enemies?"	VII	"Why do I always have to wait for you?"
II	"You never call . . . I give up!"	VIII	"You should tell me everything."
III	"I'm not going to argue with you because you know I'm right."	IX	"You should be available when I need you."
IV	"Are you listening to me?"	X	"Don't talk so much!"
V	"You should lend me money."	XI	"You're such a control freak!"
VI	"Please, don't tell me anything discouraging."	XII	"How come you're friends with _____?"

2006 World Harvest Mission

My extra commandments for my friends: _____

_____

_____

_____

Figure 4.2

"Commandments" for our workplace

I	"You are holding up my work."	VII	"Why wasn't I consulted?"
II	"Why are you always late?"	VIII	"Don't talk outside my office!"
III	"You don't recognize the great job I'm doing."	IX	"What's the big deal about being late—I work after hours?"
IV	"Why don't you work as hard as the others?"	X	"Why don't you come into work when you're sick?"
V	"His speaker phone is so loud, I can't hear myself think!"	XI	"Why don't you put things back where they belong?"
VI	"Why is there never any paper when I need this copier?!"	XII	"Why do I always have to clean up someone else's mess?!"

2006 World Harvest Mission

My extra commandments for my coworkers: _____

_____

_____

_____

Figure 4.3

"Commandments" for our family

I   "What is wrong with you?"

II   "Why are you so selfish?"

III   "Because I say so!"

IV   "I don't care what you think."

V   "Stop whining!"

VI   "Why can't you just be normal?"

VII   "Didn't I just tell you that?"

VIII   "You're late!"

IX   "It'd be nice if you helped me once in a while."

X   "I wish you wouldn't do that."

XI   "Next time, I'd appreciate it if you would . . . ."

XII   "Why are you looking at me like that?"

XIII   "I don't remember you telling me that."

XIV   "Well then, let's just get a divorce."

XV   "Oh boy, here we go again!"

XVI   "Why can't you do just this one thing?"

XVII   "Oh, I give up!"

2006 World Harvest Mission

My extra commandments for my family: _____

_____

_____

_____

Allow five minutes for group members to work through their lists. Then regain their attention and discuss the following questions:

4. Share one or two of your own commandments. Where are you most susceptible to demanding behavior? Why there?

5. What's usually the problem with statements such as the ones you've shared? What do they illustrate? Why are they so hard to avoid using?

Read the quote by Oswald Chambers below, and then discuss the questions that follow.

> *"External detachment is often an indication of a secret, vital attachment to the things we keep away from externally."*
> — Oswald Chambers

6. How have you found this to be true? In what ways have you set up laws to protect yourself from certain sins?

7. How have you seen others adversely impacted by the laws you've created? Be specific.

OPENING YOUR LIFE

In our last session we explored the barriers to love we create between us. Let's connect what we're learning in this session to that idea. As you read the following passage, realize that while Paul is referring to the Mosaic law here, the principles here apply to any laws we misuse—including those laws we create for ourselves and others.

Ask for one or more volunteers to read Galatians 3:1–5, 10–14. Then discuss the following questions:

8. How do we use our laws not only as ways to elevate ourselves, but as barriers against loving others?

9. How have your laws become a "curse" to you? How have they become barriers to loving and believing *God*, and being led by his Spirit?

10. How does your identity in Christ free you to lay down the law? Be specific.

Get into groups of three or four.

Take ten minutes to review this week's challenges and share which one you'll take on—or whether you'll take on something else God has prompted you to do instead. Close your time together in prayer. When you're done, stay quiet or move into another room, to give other pairs a chance to share and pray together. Also make plans to touch base with each other before the next session. In the space below write what you're doing in response to this week's session. May God help each of you to lay down your laws and live in his Spirit instead!

- Think again about our "commandments" lists above. In what areas are you a lawgiver rather than a law-keeper? (If you don't know, ask your spouse/coworker/friend/child/roommate—he or she will probably have a ready answer.) How are you using rules in wrong ways, and how can you apply the gospel to these situations? Think through what we have covered and how it can speak to this area.

- Here's a risky assignment, with a potentially big reward: ask those closest to you and/or those you work closely with, what one thing about you they would change. Resolve to listen to the answer and not defend yourself. The answers might surprise you. In fact, they might hurt. Take the answers you get to God; ask him to work in those areas you can't seem to get under control (and maybe couldn't even see) and allow him to change your relationship(s).

- How can you be a lawbreaker this week—the good kind? Identify one of your false laws and who specifically it's cutting you off from loving as Jesus would. Commit to putting that law—and your discomfort—aside so that you can fully be there for that person or group. Resolve instead to let the Spirit dictate how you'll respond, and to follow wherever he leads.

This week I'll "lay down the law… and leave it there" by: _____

_____

_____

_____

ADDITIONAL NOTES:

CAN WE TALK ABOUT THIS?

OVERVIEW

In this session we'll examine the distinction between being lovingly honest and being judgmental toward others, how our communication with others is affected, and how our judgmental responses expose our self-righteousness and need for repentance.

Our communication exposes our hearts, whether we want it to or not. We'll examine that truth in this session by making a clear distinction between being lovingly honest and being judgmental toward others.

It is easy to justify our judgmental responses toward others by the grain of truth contained in the statement, "I was just being honest." We are not called to practice *this* type of honesty. Being lovingly honest is for the good of others, not for our own self-glorification. Therefore, it must be coupled with forgiveness and compassion—and a deepening awareness of our own need for forgiveness and compassion—lest it become brutal.

OPENING THE DISCUSSION

1. What behavior do you find especially irritating, even (or especially) if it's something no one else cares about?

2. How do you normally react when you're irritated? What do people see? What don't they see? How long do you hold onto those feelings?

The things that irritate, anger, or offend us ultimately say more about us than about the people or things that set us off. We're called to "[speak] the truth in love" (Ephesians 4:15) and yet the "truth" part usually comes out much more easily than the love. Or, we "love" others by withholding the truth from them because we want to avoid conflict or even discomfort. But God calls us to love honestly, as Jesus loves us—not holding back on either truth or love, but knowing how and when to share what needs to be said.

OPENING THE WORD

45
MINUTES

Let's look closer at that "speaking the truth in love" passage right now and discover what we can learn from it.

Ask for one or more volunteers to read Ephesians 4:11–32, and then discuss the following questions:

3. What are the benefits to speaking the truth in love? What actions are contrasted with speaking truthfully and lovingly in this passage?

4. Reread verse 32. How does our ability to forgive affect our ability to speak the truth in love? Can "forgiveness" can be used as an escape from speaking honestly to someone who has hurt you? If so, why?

5. What do you think would happen if more of Christ's followers spoke the truth in love, that is, spoke with a compassionate honesty? Provide some specific examples of what that might look like in your own relationships.

"Our brother breaks the circle of self-deception. A man who confesses his sins in the presence of a brother knows that he is no longer alone with himself; he experiences the presence of God in the reality of the other person."
— Dietrich Bonhoeffer, *Life Together*

Let's look at a biblical example of speaking the truth in love in action and bring that example into our present-day lives.

Have a few volunteers read Galatians 1:6–10; 4:12–20; 5:7–15. Then discuss the following questions:

6. What did the Galatians do that upset Paul? How does Paul speak to them? How would you have reacted if someone had spoken to you like this?

7. What's really motivating Paul's seemingly harsh yet lovingly honest words here (see especially Galatians 1:20; 4:15, 19–20)?

*"Rebuke does not force a person
to face your judgment; it gives him an opportunity
to receive the grace of conviction, confession,
forgiveness, and repentance—to experience
the grace we also have received."*
— Paul David Tripp,
Instruments in the Redeemer's Hands

Take a minute to review the "Dishonesty" table, and then discuss the questions that follow.

Figure 5.1

Dishonesty

I can't be honest because . . . . I choose not to be honest because . . . . I won't be honest because . . .

- It won't do any good.
- It's too painful and difficult.
- He doesn't want to hear the truth.
- It's someone else's responsibility.
- She doesn't care what I think.
- I won't ever see him again.

- I don't know what to say.
- It will open a whole can of worms.
- I don't care that much.
- It won't make any difference.
- She can't handle the truth.
- He won't listen anyway.

© 2006 World Harvest Mission

8. Which of these excuses for not being honest with others are you most prone to use, and why? Are there any others you would add to this list?

9. Is it wrong to be disappointed or angry with other people sometimes? Why or why not? How should we respond, regardless?

OPENING YOUR LIFE

Sometimes even loving honesty isn't enough to prevent conflict, but we must maintain an attitude of loving honesty nonetheless. In our next session, we'll examine our need to move past being judgmental and learn to forgive as Jesus forgave us. Let's begin to move toward that idea today, by looking at someone who we know most deserves judgment—and who most needs forgiveness.

Have volunteers read Matthew 7:1–5 and Romans 2:1–8, and then discuss the following questions:

10. How does judging others reveal the deceitfulness of our own flesh, which is no less worthy of judgment than anyone else?

11. How does receiving Jesus' loving honesty and forgiveness help us to extend those same attitudes and actions to others, no matter what the situation?

Get into groups of three or four.

Take ten minutes to review this week's challenges and share which one you'll take on—or whether you'll take on something else God has prompted you to do instead. Also make plans to touch base with one another before the next session. In the space below, write what you're doing in response to this week's session.

- Is a Christian friend having a "Galatians moment"—in other words, slipping back into behaviors and/or attitudes you know the Spirit had delivered him or her from? Make time to sit down with that person to discuss. Don't go with a judgmental attitude, but with the attitude Paul had. Let your heart be broken over what's going on in your friend's life, and let *that* do the talking.

- Take a step out of your comfort zone. Reach out to a not-yet Christian friend or coworker who needs help—who maybe even is struggling with an obvious sin. Don't go with an attitude of "*now* they'll see Jesus." Hopefully they will, but don't look at it that way. Realize that person is likely starving to be shown any kind of love right now, and show him or her the best love of all— the love of Jesus. Let God use your presence however *he* wants to.

- Again, sometimes the first person who needs a dose of loving honesty is *us*. Spend time with a friend or family member and ask that person to be totally candid with you about both the good things he or she sees in you and (if he or she is a believer) areas you really haven't fully given over to God. You could even do the same for that person, if he or she is willing. Either way, make a point of praying together when you're done, inviting the Spirit to work in every issue that has been brought up.

This week I'll step deeper into loving honesty by:_____

_____

_____

_____

After ten minutes get back together, invite group members to share their challenges, and close in prayer. Pray something like this:

> *Dear God, We pray that you would help each of us to love honestly. Please address in us whichever half of that is out of balance—the love or the honesty—so that we would be able to speak the truth in love as you call us to. Amen.*

ADDITIONAL NOTES:

HOW MANY TIMES DO I HAVE TO FORGIVE?

6

OVERVIEW

In this session we will recognize that ongoing love requires both forgiveness and compassion, and we will understand how the gospel enables us to deal honestly with the hurts in our lives.

Continuing to love others, especially those close to us, will require large doses of forgiveness and compassion. Because we're still sinners, we'll contribute our fair share of sin to any situation, as well as be sinned against by others. What will keep our relationships from deteriorating or dying is ongoing forgiveness and compassion. Forgiveness allows us to acknowledge the sin of others, while blessing them by being compassionate and canceling the debt—following the example of our heavenly Father and his Son.

OPENING THE DISCUSSION

Read the note below, and then discuss the questions that follow:

A man once told his pastor, "I really hate it when my wife and I argue, because she always gets so historical." The pastor said, "Don't you mean hysterical?" The man answered, "No. I mean historical. Every time we argue, she brings up everything that I have ever done before."

1. Think of a past or present relationship that would work in the following sentence: "If it weren't for _____, _____ would be great." Explain your answer—what "historical" examples led you to come up with it?

2. How does this kind of "historical" thinking prevent *anything* from being great?

*It probably wasn't hard to think of examples just now, or to think of the people connected to those examples. "If it weren't for my spouse's (or children's) behavior, our marriage would be great." "If it weren't for certain other people in the church, church would be great." "If it weren't for our in-laws, our home life would be great." "If it weren't for other people, **life** would be great." But it's not that easy, is it? Truth is, if we took all those circumstances and people away, we'd be left with ourselves—and if it weren't for **us**, our lives would be great!*

*Thus, we need to move past the grudges or anger we feel toward others and look at them through the eyes of forgiveness and compassion—which is exactly what Jesus does with us. And that **does** make our lives great! Let's explore what that looks like.*

OPENING THE WORD

Ask for one or more volunteers to read Matthew 18:15–35, and then discuss the following questions:

3. Why do you think Peter asks his question in verse 21? What does it reveal about the condition of Peter's heart?

4. How does Jesus' response help you see the connection between forgiveness and compassion? What kind of forgiveness is Jesus looking for?

5. What's so shocking about the behavior of the servant (vv. 28–30)? In what ways are you nonetheless like him (v. 35)?

Ask for another volunteer to read James 5:11–16, and then discuss the following questions:

6. How does James connect God's compassion and forgiveness?

7. What role does confession play in forgiveness—and healing? Is confession essential for forgiveness to occur? Explain.

When we deal with hurt in our lives and the need to forgive, we can take one of two paths—the path of freedom or the path of bondage. Let's develop a better understanding of where each path takes us.

The path of freedom	The path of bondage
Choose to forgive	Choose not to forgive
Focus on Christ's forgiveness of you	Focus on your hurt
Be filled with joy and freedom	Be filled with hurt and bitterness
Become like Christ, the object of your focus	Become like the object of your bitterness

Take a minute to review the paths. Then, reread Matthew 18:15, and discuss the following questions:

8. How can the failure to forgive become a kind of bondage—for both the other person *and* you? How have you "become like the object of your bitterness"?

OPENING YOUR LIFE

*"Do I not destroy my enemies
when I make them my friends?"*
— Abraham Lincoln

Take two minutes to review the following two lists, and then discuss the question that follows:

Principles of forgiveness:

1. We must forgive because we have been forgiven.

2. We can only forgive when we see ourselves as being forgiven "big time."

3. We free ourselves and others when we forgive.

4. We become like the person we dwell on—either Christ or the person who hurt us.

5. When we forgive, on a human level we move out of the way and allow the Spirit to work.

6. When we forgive, we are not excusing sin; on the contrary, we are acknowledging the sin that people have committed against us.

Expressions of counterfeit forgiveness:

1. **Self-Protection:** "I'm just going to keep a safe distance."

2. **Record-Keeping:** "You're forgiven, but…"

3. **Minimizing the Sin:** "It was nothing…don't worry about it."

4. **Internalization:** "Maybe it's all my fault."

5. **Vengeance:** "I'll forgive you, but I'm going to make you pay first."

6. **Conditional Forgiveness:** "I'll forgive you, but you had better…"

9. Why is it so hard to forgive? What thoughts do you have when you struggle to forgive?

10. How does the gospel equip you to forgive others, even (especially) when it's hard?

Have group members get into subgroups of three or four.

*In your groups, discuss the questions below. If your discussion time brings up an issue of forgiveness you know you need to deal with, make that your challenge this week. If not, choose from one of the challenges given at the end of this session. Share the challenge you **will** take on, and make plans to touch base with each other before the next session. In the space below, write what you're doing in response to this week's session. Close your time together in prayer. When you're done, stay quiet or move into another room, to give other pairs a chance to share and pray together. May God help each of you walk deeper in his forgiveness and compassion this week!*

11. Look at the following three excuses that we may have for not forgiving others. What answers would you give to someone who gave you these excuses?

    a.   If I forgive, this person will take advantage of me, abuse me, or control me.

    b.   If I forgive, I am excusing the sin and ignoring the evil committed against me.

    c.   If I forgive, this person will become more deeply entrenched in their sin.

12. Are you currently facing a situation where *you're* giving one of the above excuses? If so, how will you take your own advice?

This week's challenges:

- When we're close to a person over a long period of time, even someone we truly love, we often build up a score of issues we've never entirely forgiven. Worse yet, we don't realize it until we have a knee-jerk reaction to something that person "always" does to us. Choose such a person and list some of your knee-jerk reactions, what triggers them, and how they're rooted in your record-keeping of past wrongs. Forgive them. Then go one step further and bless them.

- Perhaps the person you need to forgive is no longer around to hear it. You still need to forgive, however, to be free from the bondage caused by that sin. Write a letter to that person. Read it aloud and extend your forgiveness. Then tear up or burn your letter, as a symbol of having fully forgiven and released that person.

- Jesus calls us in no uncertain terms to extend his compassion and forgiveness to those in need: the homeless, the stranger, the hungry, and the incarcerated (Matthew 25:31–46). Organize a group visit (maybe *this* group) to people in the local jail; organize a social outing for children of the incarcerated; or volunteer in a soup kitchen, homeless shelter, or crisis pregnancy center. Think about how you can make this a regular practice rather than a one-time event.

This week I'll extend the forgiveness Jesus extended to me by:

_____

_____

_____

_____

ADDITIONAL NOTES:

BECOMING A HEALTHY BODY

OVERVIEW

In this session we'll place the responsibility of Christian love and relationships where it belongs—with Christ—and learn how to follow the leading of the Spirit to create and build true spiritual relationships.

We can't make the body of Christ function correctly. The good news is that it is not our job. We are *Christ's* body, not the other way around. Fortunately, the Father has not left us to figure out how to be the body of Christ on our own. Galatians 4:4–6 notes that God not only sent his Son to redeem us, but also sent us the Holy Spirit, who cries out "Abba!" within us. Through the gift of the Spirit, we are brought together as a body under one Father. Through the power of the Spirit, even relationships that seem humanly impossible not only *become* possible but become deep, loving, and lifelong.

The Spirit helps us to truly function as a body and helps us love those who don't know Jesus yet. The Spirit gives us eyes to see the needs around us, hands to reach out, and legs to travel to the ends of the earth to make the gospel known. Recognizing that we don't have to try to do this all on our own, but rather have a God who both loves **and** empowers us, frees us to serve each other and our world as Christ intends.

OPENING THE DISCUSSION

1. Think about a time you had a major illness or injury. What couldn't you do during that time without help?

2. How did your illness or injury affect others and *their* routines?

It's hard to function properly when...well, everything in our bodies isn't functioning properly. It's the same with a much larger and more important body—the church, the body of Christ.

When the body of Christ is healthy and working together, the impact reaches far beyond our group or our ministry team or our church. Conversely, when one part of the body is suffering or isn't functioning correctly, everyone's affected. Fortunately, it's not up to us to fix things. We have been brought together by the Spirit, and as we rely upon the Spirit's guidance, discipline, and healing, we not only work together as a body, but our individual rela-tionships benefit as well. Let's look deeper into this.

OPENING THE WORD

"The test case for ministry is that Jesus present by His Spirit shows up and does something only God can do . . . . The danger for us and especially for our parishioners comes when we insist on displacing the ministry of Jesus with our own ministries."
— Andrew Purves, *The Crucifixion of Ministry*

Have volunteers read John 14:15–26 and 1 Corinthians 2:9–16. Then discuss the following questions:

3. What are some of the things the Spirit teaches us, according to these passages? How do those things distinguish the church Jesus promised from "just another group of people who do good things"—maybe even *within* the church?

4. When has the Spirit reminded you of the things Jesus said to you (John 14:26)? How did you (or someone else) experience Jesus' love as you responded to that reminder?

*The Spirit is for each of us, but the Spirit isn't **just** for each of us. Let's review some passages that illustrate this point so we can better understand the complexity—and the potential—of the life the Spirit desires us all to have within the body of Christ.*

Take turns reading the following passages. Then, discuss the questions that follow.

- Acts 1:4–8
- Acts 2:11–18
- Acts 2:38–47
- Romans 5:5

- Romans 15:13
- Ephesians 2:14–22
- Ephesians 4:2–7
- Colossians 3:9–17

5. What things does the Spirit enable us to do as a church, according to these passages? List as many acts as you can.

6. If the Spirit does all *this*, what's left for *us* to do? Explain your answer.

The Spirit is a missionary, witnessing Spirit. The Spirit loves to speak about Jesus, and thus propels us to do so as well. He gives us the desire and power to speak and encourage others.

7. Reread Acts 1:8. Where are *you* most motivated by the Spirit to be a witness to his transforming power—locally (Jerusalem), beyond your regular sphere of influence (Judea/Samaria), or "to the ends of the earth"? Why?

*The Spirit creates fellowship among a bunch of sinners—us. **That** is considerable power! The Spirit first created the church at Pentecost, and now he empowers it, equips it with gifts, guides it, and governs it. The Spirit breaks down the entrenched barriers between age, race, gender, social status, education…. The Spirit unifies the church and sustains that union through love. God pours his love into our hearts by the Spirit.*

OPENING YOUR LIFE

It should be clear that as the body of Christ we all need each other. It can be tough to need each other though. It requires vulnerability, honesty, grace, sacrifice, repentance, faith, love—in other words, it requires the Spirit to continually teach us Christ. Let's examine this a little further, and the implications it has for our lives now.

Have volunteers read 1 Corinthians 12:12–27. Then discuss the following questions:

8. When have you seen the church, or members of it, rally around and support someone who was suffering? How did different parts of the body meet different areas of need?

9. How did that experience affect the person being served? How did it affect your church or ministry? How did it affect *you*?

10. Why is it so important to consider *every* part of the body of Christ important?

11. Putting all this together, what *does* the body of Christ look like when it's healthy? What does a healthy church or ministry look like? Try to come up with a concise one- or two-sentence answer as a group.

Get into groups of three or four.

Take ten minutes to review this week's challenges and share which one you'll take on—or whether you'll take on something else God has prompted you to do instead. Also make plans to touch base with one another before the next session. In the space below, write what you're doing in response to this week's session.

- Think about a spiritual friendship you're trying to develop right now—not just a relationship with another Christian, but one where you're actively pursuing Jesus together. (And if you've never thought about this, think about it now.) Now think about this: what question would you want God to answer for that person right now? How might God use you to help him or her discover that answer? Seek the Spirit's guidance in helping that friend along as you discover the answers together.

- Look for ways to support someone who is in need. Take a meal to someone who's sick. Make a phone call or a lunch appointment to encourage someone who's hurting. Take a couple of bags of groceries or a gift card to someone who's struggling financially. But as you do this, try to be very aware of how the Spirit is enabling you to see and meet needs that you ordinarily would not.

- Become an ally to an organization or cause in town that needs support. It doesn't have to be a Christian organization—in fact, what you do may have a greater impact if it isn't. How can you support your police or fire department, or an organization that specializes in showing mercy and compassion to the more marginalized members of your community? Be creative—then get involved.

This week I'll rely on the Holy Spirit to extend God's love to someone by: _____

_____

_____

_____

After ten minutes get back together and close in prayer. Pray something like this:

> *Dear God, We pray that you would help us appreciate the love you have for all people. We ask that your Spirit would reveal ways that we can work together as a body to reveal your love to our neighborhood, town, region . . . and even "to the ends of the earth." Amen.*

ADDITIONAL NOTES:

A COLLECTION OF LIGHTS

OVERVIEW

In this session we'll come to better understand that the foundation for loving others is incarnation—entering their lives and world, and bringing the life of Jesus into that world.

Jesus sums up the law and the prophets in one sentence: do to others what you would have them do to you (Matthew 7:12). We are called to a life of incarnational love, a love that enters the world of others—understanding their needs, their pain, their situation—and then brings grace through words and deeds.

We are to love in this way because it is the way we want to be loved. And we are to love in this way because it *is* the way Christ loves us. This incarnational love finds its example and motivation in the love of Christ (John 13:34; 15:12; 1 John 4:19).

OPENING THE DISCUSSION

1. Think about a time when you had to "enter someone else's world," whether it was going to a new school or workplace, meeting your spouse's parents for the first time, or taking a trip to the other side of the world. What feelings did you have at first? What helped you adapt (at least somewhat)? Share about it.

Christ came into our world. He came because he loves the entire world and because he loves each of us. It's important to maintain both sides of that perspective as we seek to live out the life of Christ in us. We need to be able to say to the outside world, and thus to each person we meet, "We will come to you. We will learn the way you do things. We will come to your world and understand you so that we can love you as Christ has loved us." When we do that, we begin to live the incarnational life of Christ.

OPENING THE WORD

*Before we explore what incarnational living means **to** us, let's better understand Jesus' incarnation and why he had to do it **for** us.*

Take turns reading Matthew 20:24–28; Luke 1:46–55; Galatians 4:4–5; Philippians 2:5–11; and 1 Timothy 1:15. Then discuss the following questions:

2. What did Jesus' incarnation accomplish? What did it require of him? *Why* did he do it? Explain your answers.

3. Jesus entered *our* world—a world filled with sin and suffering. How do these passages address our questions regarding suffering and evil?

Ask for one or more volunteers to read Mark 10:35–52, and then discuss the following questions:

4. What question here exemplifies incarnational love? (Hint: Jesus asks it twice.) What is so amazing about this question, coming from Jesus?

5. Given Jesus' attitude and actions in both these situations, what are the implications for us—whether we encounter dumbfounding pride *or* staggering need?

6. Who is it easier for you to serve, in a manner of speaking—"sons of Zebedee" or blind beggars by the roadside? Why? What do your responses to each situation reveal about the condition of your own heart?

*"O divine Master, grant that I may not so much seek
to be consoled as to console; to be understood,
as to understand; to be loved, as to love."*
— St. Francis of Assisi

Have a couple volunteers read Matthew 7:9–12 and Romans 12:9–21. Then discuss the following questions:

7. In your own words, what do these passages teach us?

8. How are these attitudes and actions evidence of Christ's life within us? Why is it so important to express Christ's incarnational love, rather than keep it to ourselves?

OPENING YOUR LIFE

Again, the life of Christ is meant to be lived out in each of his followers, through his Spirit, both individually and collectively. So let's come full circle and end with the same passage we started with today—only let's expand that passage and our view.

Take turns reading Philippians 2:1–18. Then discuss these questions.

9. Reread verse 15. What's your reaction to the idea that we can live in a way that we will "shine like stars in the universe"?

10. How does Jesus' example that we began with (vv. 6–8) assure us that this kind of shining, incarnational life is not only possible, but inevitable, as we continue to look to him?

Get into pairs.

Take ten minutes to review this week's challenges and share which one you'll take on. Especially consider one of the group options today. There's even an extra challenge today to help you and your group think it through. Again, if God is prompting you or your group to do something else, do that! Also make plans to touch base with each other before the next session. In the space below, write what you're doing in response to this week's session.

- Think of a person in your life who needs your incarnational love. How can you love him or her as you would like to be loved? Where do you need to give up your "equality"—or likely, your sense of superiority—and simply and sincerely ask, "What would you like me to do?"

- Many communities hold town festivals. Use the day as an opportunity for your group to serve and get to know others in your town. Make arrangements to set up a table or booth for that day, and then decide how you want to serve those who stop by to say hello (or better yet, walk around and meet them). Make a point of enjoying this time among the rest of your community. Don't only be generous with your resources, but also with your time and attention.

- It's no secret that many kids grow up in single-parent homes and often don't have enough time with that parent. Take a day as a group and treat those kids to a fun day of activities. Be sure to get parents' permission first; they'll probably welcome the downtime. Be specific in letting parents know where you'll be and what times you expect to be there—and keep to that itinerary. Who knows? This activity might lead to long-term mentoring relationships where group members will commit to pouring their lives into these kids.

- As a group gather food or clothing for the needy in your community. But this time, change it up a bit. Think about it: what has God given you that's been a blessing to *you*, either individually or as a group? Give *those* things away, instead of the used clothing or food that's been sitting in the closet or pantry for months. Let your sacrifice really *be* a sacrifice—a joyful sacrifice. Distribute the items yourselves if possible, or use an existing organization in the community.

This week I'll live out the incarnational life of Christ by: _____

_____

_____

_____

Leader: Note that there's an extra suggestion here, and that most of the suggestions are group-oriented. While not everyone will be ready for a team project, this might still be a good time to push people out of their comfort zones. If group members gravitate toward one idea—or again, if God's putting something else on your hearts—spend some time exploring that after wrapping up this session.

Bring the group back together after ten minutes. Ask for a few volunteers to share the challenges they're taking on. Then close in prayer, asking God to make his love incarnate in each person and visible through the challenges he's leading them to tackle.

ADDITIONAL NOTES:

GO INTO
THE WORLD

9

OVERVIEW

In this session we'll look at two general calls from Jesus: 1) come to me, and 2) go into the world—and how we can overcome our own self-made roadblocks to answering those calls.

Renewal does not end with a small group, a local church, or any other fellowship of believers. Genuine renewal brings a sweetness that, by its very nature, engenders a desire to share the gospel with others. If we have truly experienced abundant joy and peace in Jesus, how could we *not* want to share it?

Combined with this desire is the Spirit's yearning to move us out into the world. The more the Spirit changes our desires, the more we start to have Christ's concern and compassion for those who are lost and without God in the world. This lesson concentrates on this outward movement, which includes seeking to bring about mercy and justice for those who are oppressed, despised, abused, and poor.

OPENING THE DISCUSSION

Congratulations! We've made it through this study! Let's begin wrapping up the story of this season of Gospel Love by sharing about some other important stories.

1. What's your favorite story, and how does it end?

2. How have you seen the Spirit working in your life and relationships (including your fellow group members) over the last few months? How has seeing that helped *you* grow?

3. We'll explore this idea more throughout this session, but let's begin processing now. How might the Spirit's work in your life now fit into God's bigger story of redemption? In other words, how might God use what he's doing within you so others can experience the Spirit's work too?

*It's been said that we might be the only Bible some people will ever read. That's a scary thought, especially given some of the chapters that have already been written! But the good news is that God is still writing our stories. And as with any good story, God builds on what he's already done. As we follow Jesus our stories move forward, no matter how much others might or might not see. But it's the Spirit's desire **for** others to see, and respond to, his work within us. So let's finish this study by learning how to bring our inner and outer worlds closer together.*

> "Every person we encounter
> is someone who is also on the verge
> of encountering Christ incognito."
> — Robert Gelinas

OPENING THE WORD

Let's look at two calls Jesus places upon our lives, how they work together, and how we can respond to those calls more faithfully.

Ask for a couple volunteers to read Matthew 11:28–30 and Matthew 28:18–20. Then discuss the following questions:

4. What are the two interrelated calls given by Jesus (Matthew 11:28 and 28:19)? How do they complement each other?

5. Which of these two calls comes easier to you? What are the dangers in answering one of them and not the other? *Can* you answer one and not the other? Explain.

6. What does Jesus tell us about himself in these two passages? How would a deeper belief and understanding of those things help us answer his calls upon us? Be specific.

*"The Spirit of Christ is a Spirit
who longs for, and strives after, the salvation
of the souls of men, and that Spirit dwells
in them. The Spirit converts the natural instinct
into a longing for the conversion of others
which is indeed divine in its source and character."*
— Roland Allen,
The Spontaneous Expansion of the Church

Take turns reading Matthew 20:1–16 and Acts 10:9–16, 24–45. Then discuss the following questions:

7. What objections are given to others receiving grace in these passages? How does the gospel of Jesus eliminate those objections?

8. How do these passages speak to our own objections to others entering the kingdom? What should instead motivate and compel us to bring the gospel to the world?

"The Christian is a new person, living in a new world. Living in the Spirit is not an evangelistic escape from history, but a participation in the new reality of history brought by the redemptive work of Christ and the applying work of the Holy Spirit. For this reason the New Testament letters are filled with discussions of the spiritual life that interweave the heralding of the good news with topics like racial intolerance, the eating of foods used in pagan ceremonies, the position of women, family relationships, prostitution, homosexuality, the relief of poverty. To equate the spiritual with the nonphysical is completely unintelligible by New Testament standards. To isolate evangelism from the context of the world's concerns emasculates the one and ignores the other."
— Harvie Conn, *Evangelism: Doing Justice and Preaching Grace*

OPENING YOUR LIFE

*When it comes to "going out into the world"—however large or small our part of the world is—it's easy to get caught up in thinking, I can't do this, for whatever reason. We think, There are things I need to learn first; I need to accomplish more first; I don't have enough time; I need to have more credibility with that person before I open my mouth. These may well be things we need to work on. But often they're only excuses or unnecessary roadblocks we set up for ourselves. Most of the time, it's only fear of the unknown that holds us back. We make it about what we **think** we can do, rather than about what Jesus **calls** us to do and what **he promises** to do as we step out in faith.*

*The first and maybe the biggest step, then, is simply to show up—to make the most of the situation Jesus has already called us into. God's brought us through a lot already, hasn't he? More than anything, **that's** what he wants to show the people he puts in our path. Not our perfect answers or our incredible heart, but what God's done through and very arguably in spite of us—and therefore, what he can do for them, too.*

Let's conclude this study, then, by addressing our challenges and fears so we can each move forward and shine the light of Jesus to the world.

Have a couple volunteers read Matthew 5:13–16. Also, read the quote below. Then discuss the following questions:

> *"'Ye are the salt.' Jesus does not say:*
> *'You must be the salt.'"*
> — Dietrich Bonhoeffer,
> *The Cost of Discipleship*

9. Jesus says that we're *already* salt and light. How have you already seen this in some of your other relationships?

10. Among your acquaintances who really needs to "taste and see" Jesus—but you've shied away from them? What has held you back? How could developing that relationship help them—and you—to grow closer to Jesus?

11. What parts of your life need to be "tasted" more by others? What would help you become more "seasoned"? How can this group continue to support and encourage you as you begin this next chapter of your story in Christ?

Let's make our answers to that last question our challenge for this week—and beyond. Turn to a partner and share your response. Also write your commitment in the space below. Make plans to touch base with each other. We'll plan to come back together in five minutes.

This week (and beyond) I'll come to Jesus and go out into the world by: _____

_____

_____

_____

After five minutes, get back together and close in prayer. Pray something like this:

> *Dear God, Thank you for the work you've been doing in our lives, and for the relationships you've built both inside and outside this group. We ask that you would reveal more and more how each of us can be salt and light to our world. Help us continually come to you, depending on you to transform us by the work of your Spirit. In Jesus' name we pray, amen.*

ADDITIONAL NOTES:

LEADER'S GUIDE

These answers are suggestions, not definitive responses to the questions. That doesn't mean they're not helpful or accurate, but it does mean your group might come up with better—and very possibly, more personally relevant—answers. So don't rely on this guide to "feed the correct answers" to your group. That will only serve to short-circuit the impact of this course and undermine opportunities for growth in your group members' lives.

*On the other hand, the group might get stuck on one or more questions, especially depending on the maturity level of your members. In that case we're here to help. But again, don't use these answers as a crutch or a shortcut; wrestle with the questions together as a group **first** before looking at these answers.*

If you choose to use these answers as part of your regular discussion, we suggest the following format:

1. Discover. First, come up with your own complete answers to the questions using the Scripture passages, session content, diagrams, and your own personal and collective encounters with Jesus as a springboard. You need to discover the answers for yourself to get the most out of this study. As group leader, be sure to facilitate this type of learning and discussion.

2. Direct. *Now*, review, study, and discuss the suggested answers and reflections at the back of the manual.

3. Rediscover. Once you've reflected on both your answers and ours, spend time as a group talking about further ideas or questions that arise. Return to your original answers and record any new insights, thoughts, and applications.

Good luck! May God grow you together!

SESSION 1: TURNING FAITH INTO LOVE

1. Answers will vary.

2. By loving our neighbor we have done everything the law called for. Paul is not anti-law, for the law was indeed worthy to be fulfilled. And it is fulfilled by love. Thus love is greater than the entire Mosaic law. Love encompasses the law. It not only completes what the law called for, it overflows beyond it. Paul did not write, "He who loves has *obeyed* the law." *Fulfill* has the idea that when you love, the law has received above and beyond the full measure of what it required.

3. When we focus on our flesh, we take our eyes off Jesus and the gospel. When other things matter, we expend an enormous amount of energy. It takes great effort to manipulate others and protect ourselves. We become so caught up with these things that we lose sight of the gospel, and joy gets sucked out of our lives. The energy we spend on these things does not leave us much time to love others. The only thing that truly matters is that we believe the gospel and love others. When we truly serve others, our eyes are back on Jesus. All the things done out of the flesh are worth nothing; they are garbage (Philippians 3:8). The only thing that matters in our lives is that we trust and obey.

4. It is impossible to have genuine faith without having genuine love. Love is the perfect outworking of faith. To love is to be like God. Faith and hope are to be part of our lives, but love is God's character. Love is the crown jewel, the goal of faith. This is what the book of James teaches. True faith expresses itself in love for our neighbor. If you have little love, you can be sure that you have little faith. Paul says that the only thing that counts is "faith expressing itself" (NIV) or "faith working" (NASV) through love. The main idea in both of these passages is that true faith will show itself by its deeds (James) and that our deeds must flow from faith (Galatians).

5. True faith works itself out through love. True faith will show itself in a practical way in the life of the believer. Those who have faith have the power to love, and those who love others are the ones who believe. True

faith, in other words, has a practical outworking in the life of the believer.

6. Love is always a risk. It involves trust. And faith is what enables us to trust God, so that we can love as we ought and as he commands.

7. Personal examples will vary. We don't automatically look for the places where our lack of trust of God is apparent. But when we fail to love, we are also brought face-to-face with our lack of faith. At best, we'll run into both our lack of faith and lack of love simultaneously.

8. Personal examples will vary. But consider this: if love is the fulfillment of the law (Romans 13:8, Galatians 5:14), then the reverse is also true—our lack of love is an inability to fulfill the law. And thus, doing the right thing for the wrong reasons is still sin. Consider the example in Luke 11, of the Pharisee who was surprised that Jesus didn't wash before the meal. As Jesus' response indicates, it's *when* we lack love that we instead throw the law at others. *We* become people who "load people down with burdens they can hardly carry, and…will not lift one finger to help them" (Luke 11:46), who are proud of tithing because it "gets us out of" being just (v. 42), who emphasize being clean on the outside rather than the inside (v. 39)—all to make ourselves feel good. And if we try to justify ourselves at Jesus' expense, as the Pharisee did, guess who's wrong?

9. Love is the perfect outworking of faith. To love is to be like God. Faith and hope are to be part of our lives, but love is God's character. Love is the crown jewel, the goal of faith.

10–11. Answers will vary.

SESSION 2: WE'RE IN THIS TOGETHER

1. Spending time together helps get us past our "walls"; it fosters an environment of trust, then transparency, then vulnerability. Shared experiences—such as gathering together for Bible study, working together on a service project, or even hiking or picnicking—also give us opportunities to open up.

2. Answers will vary. "Fear of judgment" will almost certainly be one of them. "I've been burned before" will likely be another. Other answers won't be as overtly negative, though. The fact is, we're often so busy "doing" that we don't just stop and *be* with other people—especially those we see regularly on a Sunday morning or weeknight, for example.

3. Now that you are united with Christ, you are part of a new family. Being united with Christ unites you with everyone else who is in Christ. We now belong to each other. There is nothing holy about withdrawing from Christian company.

4. We are one body. We are all related, connected, and interdependent as members of one body. We all believe in one person, Jesus. We worship and serve the same Savior. We have one Lord. So we are one in faith. We all have the same goal, the same destination, and the same hope. We were all baptized into one body. We all underwent the same form of initiation into the church. We were all baptized into Christ (Galatians 3:27). There is only one Spirit, not a multitude of different "spirits." All believers share in the one Spirit who unifies the church. There is only one Father. We all have the same Father, who is over all, making us all part of the same family. Union with Christ brings us into union with one another. It is not as if we have to drum up this unity; we are already united! Now we just need to live out of this truth. We *are* united, so we ought to *act* united.

5. All the truths listed above concerning our unity are to be accepted by faith. Now we are called to live out of the unity we already have in Christ. We do not have to create this unity. Rather, we have to ensure that we maintain, nurture, and sustain it through loving one another. The Spirit produces in us the fruit that is needed to engender unity and love. The Spirit supplies the peace and love needed to maintain this unity, but we are commanded to make every effort to maintain it.

Life is all about relationships, and we are part of a new and united community. God calls us to be deeply involved with other people, to move toward others in love. If we are not being connected, we are not following the Spirit or the law of Christ.

6. Possible answers include the following:

Matthew 28:18–20—We are a new community of outreach. You could share something of what you're learning in this course with a not-yet Christian.

Romans 15:26—We are a new community of givers. Consider how to contribute, either financially or physically, to missionaries (like Paul) or to existing community-service groups.

2 Corinthians 1:3–5—We are a new community of comfort. When we are bereaved, God comforts us by using other believers to encourage us. We are then better able to comfort others who go through similar situations.

Ephesians 5:19—We are a new community of worship. We might consider playing a musical instrument for worship service (or in small group!).

Philippians 4:6—We are a new community of prayer. We could participate in a regular prayer meeting of friends.

Hebrews 3:13—We are a new community of encouragement. Strive each day to encourage someone to greater faith in Christ, realizing that without encouragement, a heart can become hardened in just one day.

James 1:27—We are a new community of service. You could serve by regularly helping someone who is poor, old, lonely, or oppressed.

1 John 1:7—We are a new community of fellowship. Regularly invite people to your home for meals.

7. Genuine sanctification is always connected to our relationships. To be holy we must love God and others (Matthew 22:37–40). We see how well we love God by how well we love other people. "If anyone says, 'I love God,' yet hates his brother, he is a liar. For anyone who does not love his brother, whom he has seen, cannot love God, whom he has not seen." (1 John 4:20). Thus, authentic sanctification is always connected to other people. It cannot be achieved by locking ourselves away in a closet.

8. We isolate ourselves for some of the following reasons: to punish someone else (i.e., "payback"); self-protection; fear of intimacy; self-righteousness; and laziness. When I'm not engaged with others, I'm only engaged with... *me*. Thinking a lot about both my successes and failures...the comforts that I am looking forward to...the food I want to eat...the entertainment I want to experience...the admiration of others...completing a difficult project...the affections of my spouse...wanting to be seen as more spiritual the next time, so I can admire myself...my sadness over my failure, for I am no longer worthy of my own worship...anxiety—revealing a tremendous focus on myself and an underlying fear that I will not get what I require to be happy and fulfilled...judging and criticizing others. Life in the new community is the opposite of self-absorption!

9–11. Answers will vary. Strongly encourage your group to follow through on its commitments during the week. As good as your small group is, it's usually those "offline" moments with only one or two people where they build trust and really begin to share how God is working in their lives and where he's *looking* to work next.

SESSION 3: I HAVE TO LOVE *THEM?*

1. Answers will vary.

2. We are not to resist those who are difficult to love, but serve them. We are to love and pray for those who persecute us. We are to bless those who persecute us (Romans 12:14), to not repay evil for evil (v. 17), to not take revenge (v. 19) but overcome evil with good (v. 21). If our enemy is hungry or thirsty, we are to feed him (v. 20). Often those who are difficult to love find *us* difficult to love as well, so our love at the very least confuses them and often slows them down. We are in effect a living gospel to them. We are incarnating God's radical love for them. The meaning of "heap burning coals on his head" is debated, but most agree that Paul has something positive and beneficial in mind—possibly leading them to repentance.

Jesus' exhortation to be perfect refers to the depth of love we ought to have. He is not setting before us a "perfection" that is either attainable or unattainable. Rather, he is exhorting us to love like God, who loves those who are difficult to love. This is the righteousness that exceeds that of the Pharisees, who do not love like this. In Luke 6:36, we are called to be merciful as God is merciful. Jesus points us to an otherworldly kind of love, a love that does not characterize relationships in this world. Jesus is referring to a way of life that is different from the way most people relate to one another. The rubber meets the road not when we deal graciously with people who are kind to us, but when we love those who hate and despise us.

3. Jesus was unwilling to save himself; instead he made himself vulnerable to excruciating pain and humiliation, to the point of enduring the cross, in order to save us and bring us back into a right relationship with him. Every time we love someone, we make ourselves vulnerable. We open our lives to their rejection, anger, dismissal, or judgment. Yet we also open our lives to their acceptance, kindness, responsiveness, and encouragement. Thus, we love with the hope of greater intimacy.

4. The world, the flesh, and the devil will continually challenge any vulnerability that we allow in our lives. To love we have to be vulnerable, and this risk may be questioned by those who are difficult to love. So we will face temptations, such as the following: If you remain vulnerable, you will be powerless. If you live by faith and place yourself in the Father's hands, no one will look after you. If you love, no one will be there for you, and no one will meet your needs. If you are vulnerable, you may save others, but you will not save yourself.

5. The church at Sardis achieved a reputation through false fruit, deeds that looked good on the outside, but were in fact hollow and plastic. Imitation fruit—and thus, a false reputation—can be produced without faith, repentance, and the Spirit. Thus it is important to identify false fruit so that we can grow in genuine love.

Consider the proverb, "The prudent keep their knowledge to themselves" (Proverbs 12:23). Why is this the case? They conceal knowledge because they have faith. They know that they are not God. They do not glorify themselves, so they don't tell people everything they know. They are not confident of their own opinions. Moreover, since they live by faith, they know the danger of imitation fruit and its resulting lack of love. They don't conceal knowledge in order to dazzle everyone with their insight at just the right moment.

6. Personal examples will vary. Our world operates by conditional love— return love for love and good for good. Tax collectors and pagans love those who are kind to them. Jesus' point is that it is no great accomplishment to have this kind of discriminating love. Like the tax collectors, we often impose certain conditions on love. I will love you if…I will love you but…I will love you while…I will love you when….

7. Likewise, our first reaction when we are suffering is usually not "How can I love?" but rather, "How can others love me?" The strong temptation when we are suffering is to stop loving others. We are tempted to judge those who are causing the suffering or persecution and to think that we are better. We are tempted to think that God has forgotten about us or has turned against us. We are tempted to try to take control of the situation and change the stones we find in our lives into bread. Thankfully, we have a great high priest, Jesus, who knows the intense temptations that come from suffering; thus he is merciful and sympathetic toward us in our suffering.

8. Personal responses will vary. The bigger issue is that we *can't* love like this. Not on our own. However, we are reconciled to Christ because of his supernatural love for us, despite *our* sin (Romans 5:8). And as God's love has been poured into our hearts through the Holy Spirit given to us (Romans 5:5), we too are enabled to love even those who have hurt us immeasurably or who seem unlovable.

9. Answers will vary.

10. Judgment hurts, no matter which direction it travels. And because it's coming from flawed people like us, that judgment is never entirely accurate. We find our way around the planks in our own eyes in order to find the speck of sawdust in our brother's eye (Matthew 7:3). Thus, we must be merciful as our Father is merciful, not judging lest we be judged (Luke 6:36–37).

11. We have nothing to recommend ourselves to God. Even if we were humanly wise, or influential, or rich (1 Corinthians 1:26), it is all garbage compared to knowing Jesus (Philippians 3:8). Every one of us is weak, lowly, and despised (1 Corinthians 1:27–28), but Jesus has become our wisdom, righteousness, holiness, and redemption (v. 30). This is every bit as true—at least potentially—with every other person we'll ever meet. We must strive to recognize Christ's ongoing work in that other person.

12. Answers will vary.

SESSION 4: LAY DOWN THE LAW . . . AND LEAVE IT THERE

1. Answers will vary.

2–3. Possible answers include the following:

Mark 3:1–6—The Pharisees drew life from conforming to a set of laws. Some of these rules concerned what they could or could not do on the Sabbath. They got life by keeping a set of laws so they could feel good about themselves, gain the respect of others, and condemn others. This way of "life," however, concerns watching others and looking for ways to accuse them (v. 2). It only works if you can demonstrate that you are better than others. In verse 4, Jesus confronts them, "Then Jesus asked them, 'Which is lawful on the Sabbath: to do good or to do evil, to save life or to kill?' " Apparently the Pharisees thought the latter—in verse 6 they plot to murder Jesus! For all their talk about the Sabbath, they break the Sabbath in the worst possible manner.

Luke 7:36–50—Simon's false law is "Do not associate with sinful people." He uses this rule to excuse himself from loving the woman. He also uses it to condemn Jesus. Simon, with his misuse of laws, is the real lawbreaker. Jesus tells him that he has little love (v. 44–46), in contrast to the woman's lavish demonstration of love for Jesus. Simon is shown to be condemning and distant, while both Jesus and the woman are portrayed as loving.

John 12:1–7—Judas misuses a law about the use of money to condemn Mary. He makes her appear unloving and wasteful. Judas also uses it to make himself look good—to appear frugal, wise, and concerned for the poor. With one law, Judas has made someone else look bad and himself look good. In fact, Judas is a lover of money (v. 6). We often condemn in others the things we struggle with most. Jesus, however, looks at the heart and the circumstances. "Leave her alone," Jesus replies. "It was intended that she should save this perfume for the day of my burial" (v. 7).

4. Answers will vary.

5. Usually, these statements are demanding and illustrate wrong uses of laws or rules. When we use laws incorrectly, we say, "Life to me, death to you." They demonstrate a lack of trust in the Spirit. A correct use of laws says the opposite: "Death to me, life to you." It is wrong to use rules or commands for selfish reasons, for self-righteousness and self-gratification. We use them correctly when we use them for the good of others, when we say, "The commands of God call me to lay down my life for this person."

6. Answers will vary. We often create laws to protect ourselves from sins of license. Then, because it still stems from self, we fall instead into legalism. Because often these rules or laws are good in and of themselves, it is easy to fall into the trap of thinking that all uses of these laws are good. We end up justifying ourselves; meanwhile, we leave a trail of death behind us. The abuse of laws comes from powerful idols; thus change is difficult.

7. Answers will vary. We use laws or rules wrongly when we use them to gain control, power, order, status, or reputation (by defending, blaming, credit-mongering, or comparing). These laws are not a list of "rights" I can demand from others. Rather, they are laws for how I am to treat others. So when we complain, criticize, and provoke our spouses for reading the map incorrectly, we become a lawbreaker. There is nothing immoral about reading a map incorrectly; however, there's something very wrong with our anger and criticism.

8–10. We use laws to stay out of relationships, or at least to put distance in them, and to feel justified in doing so. With this way of life others are the lawbreakers; we do not have to repent or die. If we can bring about obedience through nagging, then we can get along without faith and the Spirit. Why pray when we can force and compel others? If we live this way, then we do not need the gospel. We have, experientially, rejected Christ's saving work on our behalf, and thus we live as if we were still under the curse of the law.

SESSION 5: CAN WE TALK ABOUT THIS?

1–2. Answers will vary.

3. The benefits to speaking the truth in love include increased maturity in Christ—maturity not just for us or the person across from us, but for the entire body of Christ. Speaking the truth in love is contrasted here with cunning, craftiness, and deceitful scheming. We are by nature "people-pleasers" and "people-judges" and therefore avoid speaking the truth in love. We may justify our avoidance on the basis of not wanting to hurt the other person, but the truth is that we do not want to risk further hurt for ourselves. Or we may justify our interference by claiming that the other person needs to hear what we have to say, but the truth is that we want to pass judgment on them and put them in their place.

4. True forgiveness places others higher than ourselves. We know the depth of our sin, and therefore do not hold another's sin against them. If our desire for relief from conflict is greater than our desire for a genuine healing of the relationship, then a quickness to forgive may only be an attempt to avoid more hurt in the relationship. To forgive when we really have not come to grips with how we have been hurt is like covering over an infected sore. Forgiveness is not sweeping our hurts under the rug. It includes honestly recognizing where we have been hurt. Forgiveness does not exclude speaking honestly to the person who harmed us.

5. There would be more constructive conflicts and fewer destructive conflicts. Disagreements openly expressed to the appropriate person would be less likely to grow and fester into gossip.

6–7. Paul is upset because the Galatians are turning to a false gospel (1:6). After beginning with the Spirit, they are now trying to attain their goal (living the Christian life) by the flesh (3:3). They are in the process of rejecting the gospel that has been clearly preached to them, and of turning away from a life dependent on the Spirit. Paul grieves because of their spiritual danger, but he handles this particular problem with directness and candor (4:17–20). There is urgency in his appeal because of the seriousness of the problem he is confronting and because of his concern for them (3:1; 5:7–12). Nevertheless, though he is speaking honestly to them, Paul affirms his love and respect for them (4:19), while rejecting the error and false way of life into which they have fallen. Although we may bristle at such words at first, we should welcome them. The wounds from a friend are always better than the kisses of an enemy (Proverbs 27:6).

8. Answers will vary.

9. No! They are sinners just like you. Sin makes life in general, and relationships in particular, messy. We were not created to live like this—in an evil and hurting world. Neither are we to suppress our emotions or become emotionally detached from people. However, disappointment in others or anger is not a characteristic we commonly see in Paul. In our lives, more often than not, what we experience is sinful disappointment and anger because people do not live up to our high expectations.

We can stuff our hurts deep down inside, but they will leak out in other ways—depression, sickness, self-pity, anger, bitterness, or gossip. We were created to be honest with one another. Because we are all sinners, however, we always need to temper our honesty with compassion and forgiveness.

10. The things we judge others for are usually the things we have problems with in our own lives. We have little awareness of our hypocrisy because we are self-deceived. Our pride blinds us to the plank in our own eyes. I will be judged by the same standard I use to judge others. It is too easy when dealing with another person to fall into the trap of self-righteousness. Although we are all sinners, I am often tempted to think that I am not as great a sinner as someone else.

11. Jesus is patient, kind, and tolerant toward us in order to lead us to repentance. We should show a similar tolerance, kindness, and patience in our dealings with others. We should be like Jesus in his qualities of honesty, forgiveness, and compassion. The lack of these qualities in our lives exposes our self-righteousness and our need of God's mercy. One specific way we can respond to others instead of judging them is to ask questions. We need to ask questions because we do not know all the details of any situation, and we are often wrong about people. We ask questions so that we can know how to bring grace to a particular situation and minister to people's real needs. When I need to be honest with another person, I must first repent of my own sins, and then go to them, seeing myself as the bigger sinner.

SESSION 6: *HOW* MANY TIMES DO I HAVE TO FORGIVE?

1. Answers will vary.

2. Holding onto others' failures and sins doesn't make them, or us, better. It builds walls between us. It puts us in bondage to those feelings of hurt, indignation, and disappointment. It makes us less like Jesus, and it makes our relationship with him feel distant as well.

3. Peter feels that he needs some clarification on the issue of forgiveness. He asks a "yes, but" question. Yes, but how often do I need to forgive my sister or brother? Yes, but what if they keep sinning against me? Do I still have the obligation to take the initiative in forgiving them? Yes, but what if they keep on doing the same thing again and again? Yes, but do you know what they are really like? Yes, but is there not a limit?

The frustration in Peter's question is palpable. He's essentially asking Jesus when is it okay to stop turning the other cheek to my brother and just *smack* him back? When is it okay to exercise my right to justice and see that he pays for what he's done? The common teaching of the day was that you only had to forgive someone three times. Peter ups this to seven, as if to say, "I'll double you and raise you one. That should be good odds to live by. With these odds, I should be able to win this discussion." We must be aware that Peter is not being generous here. His question betrays his heart. We do not need to search far to find Peter's heart attitude in our own hearts.

4. Jesus is looking for forgiveness from the heart. This type of heart forgiveness cannot be given out of a sense of duty. A hypocrite can tithe, attend church, preach, and do his work, but he cannot forgive those who grievously sin against him. Duty, self-effort, and self-discipline will not cut it. Why? Because Jesus is looking for forgiveness from the heart— even for those who cripple us. And that will not come without a heart of compassion. We need the heart of Jesus in order to forgive from the heart.

People say they discipline themselves to read the Bible, get up early, pray, or have family devotions. But who says, "I have disciplined myself to forgive others from the heart"? Forgiveness comes when we receive into our own lives by faith what God has done for us. We had an enormous debt, but it has been canceled. When that truth becomes big in our hearts and lives, then we will be empowered by the Spirit to forgive. Only through the gospel can we receive the motivation and the power to forgive others.

5. Our first reaction may be, "How could this servant turn so quickly into such a monster? This man deserves to be punished for his hatred, hardness, and lack of compassion!" Perhaps we respond indignantly, as David did when Nathan told him the story of the stolen lamb, "How could that man act so shamefully and take a poor man's only lamb? He must be put to death!" (see 2 Samuel 12). But like the parable Nathan told to David, this one too has a twist, and this time we are the ones who are caught. We are the ones who have been forgiven a huge debt, yet we are those who go and exact justice and vengeance from others.

We can see ourselves clearly in this parable. Many times we "throttle" and "choke" people who have not even sinned against us. Never mind crippling debts; we attack, nag, and condemn others because they have broken some of our pet rules or offended our scruples. We are out for "justice." If we are not living with the reality that God in Christ has forgiven our great debts, we will do exactly as the wicked servant does in the parable. We will say, "I'm not going to stand for this. I'm going to settle accounts. It's payback time—I'm in seek-and-destroy mode. Never mind what God has done for me."

6. God's compassion is central to love and central to the gospel because compassion moves us into the lives of others. It ultimately moved Jesus to die for us so that we could receive God's forgiveness. In James's example here, that compassion specifically encourages us to move toward others in a spirit of faith, prayer, and openness to God. Because of that spirit of compassion, those who have sinned are forgiven and encouraged to confess their sins to one another so that they may be healed.

7. Confession exposes our sin to the light of the gospel so that we may be transformed and healed. However, we must not wait for someone else to "own up" to what they've done to us. For that matter, it's important to note that forgiveness doesn't mean an automatic restoration of a damaged relationship. Forgiveness doesn't mean reconciliation and a restoration of trust. You can genuinely forgive and yet not restore a relationship, nor trust the person again with your life and heart. Forgiveness is an offer of mercy—to yourself and to the other person. Forgiveness is merciful to you, for it frees you from the bondage of the other person's sins. It is merciful to the other person, for it offers them an opportunity for confession and repentance. Depending on the circumstance, your forgiveness—and the confession of your own part in the matter—may open the door to much more. It may offer reconciliation, which over time may also lead to a restoration of trust.

8. Personal examples will vary. The fear of being taken advantage of again by those who have offended you can control you and determine your future responses to them. You may begin distancing yourself from them or even going out of your way to avoid them. The result is that your lack of forgiveness begins to control you and you are enslaved by their sin—and your own.

9. Forgiveness is so difficult because we are choosing to pay down someone else's debt—the one that has been incurred by their sins against *us*. Our fallen hearts want justice, and thus we will rationalize why we

believe forgiveness is wrong in this situation. We think, *They will take advantage of me. They will abuse my love. If I keep on forgiving, they will keep hurting me. I will become a doormat. It really hurt. They do all the sinning; I do all the forgiving. I don't want to appear weak—that's what they want. They don't even realize how much they have hurt me. I don't deserve to be treated this way; it's not fair. They are so hard-hearted and unrepentant. This happens all the time—they don't care what I think. It would be nice to have a bit of vindication or vengeance instead. I have to keep on forgiving them. To forgive exposes my own heart and similar sins that I am forgiving—so let's forget the whole thing!*

10. Answers will vary.

11. **(a) If I forgive, this person will take advantage of me, abuse me, or control me.** However, exactly the opposite is true. When we do not forgive, we distance ourselves and go out of our way to avoid people, or we begin to gossip about them. These are all indications of how the other person is beginning to control us, and how we are actually in a kind of bondage to them. When I forgive repeatedly, from the heart, I am no longer in bondage to the other person's sins. I am free to love them and the Spirit is free to work in me and in them.

(b) If I forgive, I am excusing the sin and ignoring the evil committed against me. Again, the opposite is true. Forgiveness is in fact acknowledging and facing up to the real evil that other people commit. We should not tell people, "Hey, it's not a big deal." Rather, we should say something like, "I do forgive you." Forgiveness is not forgetting what others have done. It is saying we will no longer hold their sin to their account. It means we have closed the books. (However, forgetting may come eventually.) Thus, forgiveness does not ignore sin or its consequences, nor does it tell the offender, "It was no big deal."

(c) If I forgive, this person will become more deeply entrenched in their sin. Actually, the opposite often occurs. When Christ prays that God will forgive his persecutors, the centurion is converted. Likewise, Stephen prays for the forgiveness of his persecutors, and Saul is converted shortly afterwards. God not only forgives, he also works through those who are forgiving. When we repeatedly forgive, we are no longer in bondage to the sins of others. We are then freed to genuinely love them, and the Spirit is free to work in them without hindrance. Finally, through the process of forgiving and loving, we become more like our great King who is forgiving and compassionate.

12. Answers will vary.

SESSION 7: BECOMING A HEALTHY BODY

1–2. Answers will vary.

3. The Spirit of truth is our advocate (John 14:16–17). The Spirit teaches us the thoughts of God himself, which can only be spiritually discerned (John 14:17; 1 Corinthians 2:11–15). The Spirit teaches us that we are sons of God in Christ (John 14:18–20). The Spirit reminds us of everything Jesus has said (John 14:26). In fact, the Spirit gives us the mind of Christ (1 Corinthians 2:16). Even the "good things" we do, apart from God's will, are based in us and thus sinful. Through the Spirit we are able to discern and perform the will of the Father, and to see that we are created in Christ Jesus to do the *true* good works that God himself prepared in advance for us to do (Ephesians 2:10).

4. Answers will vary.

5. The Spirit gives us power to witness, from our doorstep to the ends of the earth (Acts 1:8). That witnessing will not only manifest itself as evangelism (Acts 2:38–41), but as prophecy (Acts 2:17–18), a love for one another that's openly expressed and clearly visible to others (Acts 2:40–41), full generosity with the material things God has entrusted to us (Acts 2:44–45), open praise for God (Acts 2:47), visible hope and love (Romans 5:5), joy and peace (Romans 15:13), unity across every kind of cultural barrier (Ephesians 2:19).

6. We are to wait for the Spirit's power. We already have it within us, but if we run out ahead of the Spirit's leading we will not have the power we

need when we need it. In the meantime, we are to be humble, gentle, and patient with one another, maintaining our unity in the Spirit (Ephesians 4:2–3). We are to maintain our peace in Christ (Colossians 3:15) as we humbly wait.

7. Answers will vary. If group members get stuck, direct them to think about the people whose situations move their hearts. Is it someone they know closely? An urban ministry? Do they enjoy sponsoring children in poverty overseas? Once the people are identified, their location becomes much more obvious.

Instead of political power, which the disciples were evidently hoping for in Acts 1:6, Jesus promised his followers a far greater power. It would be a power of far greater influence, yet not for their own advancement, but for the good of others. This desire of the Spirit encompasses the world— from Jerusalem to the ends of the earth. The change brought about in the disciples by the Spirit was nothing less than extraordinary. They were changed from being fearful, insular, and limited in their vision, to being bold, outward, and visionary.

8–9. Answers will vary. Examples might include the following: A new kind of unity within the church; people became more loving and forgiving toward one another; that person's life was transformed, as he or she broke out of spiritual/emotional/financial bondage; it opened a brand-new door to ministry that the church had previously been unaware of.

10. To say, "I don't need you!" (1 Corinthians 12:21) is the height of arrogance. Jesus values every one of us, in all our sins, faults, and weaknesses. To accept that truth and to extend it to others is the Spirit's desire for each of us. God has created each of us uniquely. To ignore certain people or their giftedness is to present a lopsided, crippled body of Christ. Leaders need those who show mercy and vice versa. Servants need teachers, who need givers, who need administrators, and so on. Those struggling with poverty need those struggling with pride—and given Christ's heart for the poor, the reverse is probably far more true. Every interaction within the body of Christ is an opportunity for the Spirit to manifest his power to the world.

11. Answers will vary. But perhaps the best definition, although it's a bit longer than two sentences, comes from Ephesians 4:11–16:

> It was he who gave some to be apostles, some to be prophets, some to be evangelists, and some to be pastors and teachers, to prepare God's people for works of service, so that the body of Christ may be built up until we all reach unity in the faith and in the knowledge of the Son of God and become mature, attaining to the whole measure of the fullness of Christ.
>
> Then we will no longer be infants, tossed back and forth by the waves, and blown here and there by every wind of teaching and by the cunning and craftiness of men in their deceitful scheming. Instead, speaking the truth in love, we will in all things grow up into him who is the Head, that is, Christ. From him the whole body, joined and held together by every supporting ligament, grows and builds itself up in love, as each part does its work.

SESSION 8: A COLLECTION OF LIGHTS

1. Answers will vary.

2. The incarnation exemplifies the humility of God. The King and Creator of the universe comes into our world without majesty and splendor. He comes to Bethlehem as a dependent baby. "But you, Bethlehem Ephrathah, though you are small among the clans of Judah, out of you will come for me one who will be ruler over Israel, whose origins are from of old, from ancient times" (Micah 5:2). This love does not enter just any world, but a world of sin, misery, and death. Jesus leaves his throne above and incarnates into our world. He comes to us. He comes to be one of us and to identify with our world. Even though he is the Creator, he comes into our world to help us.

We must always connect the incarnation with the cross, lest we lose the

New Testament focus on the death and resurrection of Christ. Jesus came to die. He came to give his life in order to save sinners and restore the cosmos. "For this reason he had to be made like his brothers in every way, in order that he might become a merciful and faithful high priest in service to God, and that he might make atonement for the sins of the people" (Hebrews 2:17). Jesus came to destroy the works of the devil (1 John 3:8). His name *Jesus* means that he will save his people from their sins (Matthew 1:21). We must always recognize that the incarnation is closely connected with the cross.

3. Jesus comes into a world of suffering. He comes and suffers with us. All our questions about suffering must be seen in light of the great answer given in Christ. God does not stand removed or far off from our fallen and painful world. We will never figure out the place and purposes of our suffering, but we can know that God is with us.

Leader, this is a good place to introduce personal examples of suffering and brokenness, together with explanations as to how these situations have helped you minister to others.

---

4. "What do you want me to do for you?" What an amazing question from the King and Sustainer of the universe. While many people are telling the blind man to keep quiet, Jesus enters the world of Bartimaeus. Incarnational love starts with the remarkable question, "What do you want me to do for you?" (Mark 10:51). This love enters into the world of others for their good. It is surprising, even shocking. This question is always on the heart and lips of a servant.

"What do you want me to do for you?" may have been an even more amazing question to ask James and John (v. 36). Our response to them probably would have been more like, "Who do you think you *are*?" And yet Jesus—who would have had more right to ask the latter question than anyone—ignores their arrogance and presumption and once again comes in the form of a servant, setting aside his rightful claims as God (Philippians 2:6–7).

5. It is a great struggle to ask, "What can I do for you?" Often we almost choke when asking someone this question, for it raises other questions in our minds: What if they overwhelm me with their problems? What if I can't get rid of them? If I ask this now, will I have to ask it again… and again? Will I lose control of this situation? What if they ask me to do something I am not prepared to do? If I help this person, who'll help *me*? What if I can't help them? What if I don't know what to say or how to answer them?

Jesus' question is so difficult for us to ask because incarnational love is contrary to how we usually live. It is much easier to either maintain our distance or to meddle. Instead, incarnational love enters the world of others at the point where they are lonely, weak, suffering, needy, or broken. Instead of interfering with other people's lives, incarnational love asks whether they want our help.

6. Answers will vary.

7. In every situation, treat others as you would want to be treated. Go and do to others what you would have them do to you. In everything, put yourself in the other person's shoes, and then act in the way you would like others to act toward you. In all things, incarnate yourself and enter into the world of others; see things from their perspective; seek to understand their language, their life, their pain, and their joy. Then love them as you would like to be loved if you were in the same situation. This incarnational love sums up the law and the prophets.

8. We cannot love people until we have entered their world. Incarnation must come first. Before we can speak into others' lives or help them, we need to understand their situations. We tend to barge in without understanding, to give "help" when help is not wanted, or to think that what worked for us will automatically work for others. Barging in or remaining aloof are both tactics for remaining distant in relationships. The first step in genuine love must always be incarnation.

The Matthew 7 passage is another way of summing up the entire Mosaic law: love your neighbor as yourself (Leviticus 19:18; Romans 13:9; Galatians 5:14; James 2:8). It expresses the sum total of our calling —nothing more, nothing less. Our differences with other believers do not sum up the law and prophets. Knowing the intricacies of theology or having correct theology does not sum up the law and the prophets. Witnessing to others or having regular devotions does not sum up the law. What does sum up the Old Testament law? It is incarnational love.

9. Answers will vary.

10. Paul tells us to have the same mindset as Jesus (Philippians 2:5)—not to try, but to do. Furthermore, he states in verse 13, "it is *God* who works in you to will and to act according to his good purpose." We can't live the kind of life Jesus calls us to on our own; thankfully, we were never meant to. Paul points to his own example, indicating that only because of Christ's example and power is he too able to be "poured out like a drink offering on the sacrifice and service coming from your faith," yet "glad and rejoic[ing] with all of you" (v. 17).

SESSION 9: GO INTO THE WORLD

1–2. Answers will vary.

3. Answers will vary. The gospel loses its sweetness when we do not share it. We must first preach the gospel to ourselves, then go and preach it to others. Isaiah writes in Isaiah 60:1–3, "Arise, shine, for your light has come, and the glory of the Lord rises upon you....Nations will come to your light, and kings to the brightness of your dawn." The gospel is attractive—the most attractive thing in the universe. It is beautiful; it brings light; it lifts burdens; it brings the power of God; it is good news.

Leader, one way of prompting your group to share is to ask how much their desire to speak to others about Jesus is growing. This may be a good test to see some benefits from this course—has their desire to bring grace to others grown?

---

4. Jesus calls every follower to do two things: come to me, and go into the world. The gospel must first come to us before it can go out to others. Before we can go into the world we must come to Jesus. Once we have come to Jesus, then we are to go into the world.

5. We can only speak of what we have seen and heard, otherwise our words are empty. Then we go, confident in the power of God, for we have seen God change us. We go in weakness, for we know we have many "planks"—many remaining sins. This process is ongoing: as we continually come to Jesus, we continually go into the world.

6. Jesus is the one who gives us rest. In our flesh we don't rest by getting the work done; we move right on to the next work. As we come to Jesus we find our rest in him, for his yoke is easy and his burden is light. Jesus has all authority on heaven and earth, and it is with that authority that he commissions us to go into the world. No matter how far Jesus takes us, he is surely with us, to the end of this age.

7. In the parable in Matthew 20:1–16, people are envious because God is gracious. They believe that they have a right to be treated by God in a special way because they are different from everyone else. They have put themselves in the category of those who have worked long and hard all day, so they resent God's forgiveness and grace to others. In the end they believe that "Grace is for people like us, who have worked long and hard." Jesus did not act according to the belief that some people were better than others! He came into the world to eat with sinners, to call tax collectors, to touch lepers, to let prostitutes touch him. Common people were called to be his disciples, not the religious leaders.

The Jewish believers in Acts 10 had the same problem. Their instinctive reaction was to think, "These Gentiles do not have a history of keeping the Mosaic law. God has been with us for ages, but we are not too sure about these Gentile sinners. They do not seem to have done enough, or worked hard enough. We are the ones who have worked through the heat of the day." Even Peter had to be shown a vision from heaven to convince him that grace is for everyone. Grace does not stop with us.

The Lord calls his church to embrace its missionary, evangelistic, and social calling.

8. If we believe that God is gracious toward sinners, then we have to acknowledge that we ourselves are sinners, undeserving of anything. Renewal does not end with our small group, our church, or any other gathering of believers. The more Christ and his Spirit change our desires, the more we will have his concern for those who are lost and without God in this world. Those who are forgiven much, love much (Luke 7:47).

The love of God now compels us (2 Corinthians 5:14). We tell other people about the things we are excited about. The kingdom is coming, bringing joy, life, love in our hearts, freedom, redemption from sin—how can we not tell others about this? To hoard the good news is to become dull, passionless, hard, and critical. If we miss the mandate that the gospel is to go into the world, we will become an ingrown church, one that has turned in on itself, one where the community is saying "Grace is only for people like us."

9–11. Answers will vary. But encourage everyone in your group to share their answers, no matter how overwhelming or insignificant those answers might feel. Give the group, and the Spirit, the opportunity to address each person's concerns and the visions God is placing on each of their hearts. And may God bless each of you as you go out in his love!

mission
grace through you

At Serge we believe that mission begins through the gospel of Jesus Christ bringing God's grace into the lives of believers. It also sustains us and empowers us to go into different cultures bringing the good news of forgiveness of sins and new life to those whom God is calling to himself.

As a cross-denominational, reformed, sending agency with 200 missionaries on over 25 teams in 5 continents, we are always looking for people who are ready to take the next step in sharing Christ, through:

- **Short-term Teams:** One to two-week trips oriented around serving overseas ministries while equipping the local church for mission
- **Internships:** Eight-week to nine-month opportunities to learn about missions through serving with our overseas ministry teams
- **Apprenticeships:** Intensive 12–24 month training and ministry opportunities for those discerning their call to cross-cultural ministry
- **Career:** One- to five-year appointments designed to nurture you for a lifetime of ministry

Grace at the Fray   Visit us online at: www.serge.org/mission

www.newgrowthpress.com

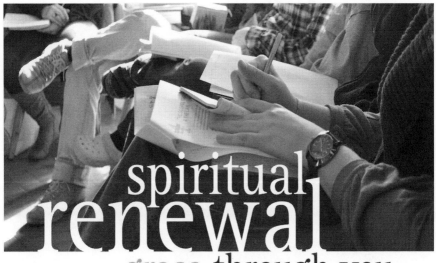

spiritual renewal
grace through you

Disciples who are motivated and empowered by grace to reach out to a broken world are handmade, not mass-produced. Serge intentionally grows disciples through curriculum, discipleship experiences, and training programs.

Curriculum for Every Stage of Growth

Serge offers grace-based, gospel-centered studies for every stage of the Christian journey. Every level of our materials focuses on essential aspects of how the Spirit transforms and motivates us through the gospel of Jesus Christ.

- 101: The Gospel-Centered Series
  (The Gospel-Centered Life, The Gospel-Centered Community)
- 201: The Gospel Transformation Series
  (Gospel Identity, Gospel Growth, Gospel Love)
- 301: The Sonship Course and Serge Individual Mentoring

Gospel Renewal for You

For over 25 years Serge has been discipling ministry leaders around the world through our Sonship course to help them experience the freedom and joy of having the gospel transform every part of their lives. A personal discipler will help you apply what you are learning to the daily struggles and situations you face, as well as, modeling what a gospel-centered faith looks and feels like.

Training to Help You Disciple Better

Serge's discipler training programs have been refined through our work with thousands of people worldwide to help you gain the biblical understanding and practical wisdom you need to disciple others so they experience substantive, lasting growth in their lives. Available for onsite training or via distance learning, our training programs are ideal for ministry leaders, small group leaders or those seeking to grow in their ability to disciple effectively.

 Grace at the Fray   Visit us online at www.serge.org/mentoring

www.newgrowthpress.com

curriculum for
every stage of
growth
grace through you

Every day around the world, Serge teams help people develop and deepen the living, breathing, growing relationship with Jesus that the gospel promises. We help people connect with God in ways that are genuinely grace-motivated and that increase their desire and ability to reach out to others. No matter where you are along the way, we have a series that is right for you.

101: The *Gospel-Centered* Series

Our *Gospel-Centered* series is simple, deep, and transformative. Each *Gospel-Centered* lesson features an easy-to-read article and provides challenging discussion questions and application questions. Best of all, no outside preparation on the part of the participants is needed! They are perfect for small groups, those who are seeking to develop "gospel DNA" in their organizations and leaders, and contexts where people are still wrestling with what it means to follow Jesus.

201: The *Gospel Transformation* Series

Our *Gospel Transformation* studies take the themes introduced in our 101 level materials and expand and deepen them. Designed for those seeking to grow through directly studying Scripture and working through rich exercises and discussion questions, each *Gospel Transformation* lesson helps participants grow in the way they understand and experience God's grace. Ideal for small groups, individuals who are ready for more, and one-on-one mentoring, *Gospel Identity, Gospel Growth*, and *Gospel Love* provide substantive material, in easy-to-use, manageable sized studies.

The *Sonship* Course and Individual Mentoring from Serge

Developed for use with our own missionaries and used for over 25 years with thousands of Christian leaders in every corner of the world, Sonship sets the standard for whole-person, life transformation through the gospel. Designed to be used with a mentor, or in groups ready for a high investment with each other and deep transformation, each lesson focuses on the type of "inductive heart study" that brings about change from the inside out.

 Grace at the Fray   Visit us online at www.serge.org/resources